MINDSHIFT

Catalyzing Change in Christian Education

EDITED BY

LYNN E. SWANER,

DAN BEERENS,

AND

ERIK ELLEFSEN

Printed in the United States of America

25 24 23 22 21 20 19 1 2 3 4 5 6

Edited by Swaner, Lynn E., Beerens, Dan, and Ellefsen, Erik

MindShift: Catalyzing change in Christian education

ISBN 978-1-58331-559-0
eISBN 978-1-58331-515-6

Catalog#: 6677 print,
          e6677 eBook

Designer: Vincent Yorke
Copyeditor: Elsie Wright

Association of Christian Schools International
731 Chapel Hills Drive • Colorado Springs, CO 80920
Member Care: 800.367.0798 • www.acsi.org

TABLE OF CONTENTS

Introduction

Lynn E. Swaner (with Beth Green)

As an educator, you've probably been there before—the conference or seminar is over after a very long day, and all you can think about is returning to your hotel room to collapse for a few hours before the next day begins. But as you head through the lobby, you spot a small group of colleagues out on the patio and decide to say a quick good night. When you approach and they pause mid-conversation to greet you warmly, someone from the group pulls up a chair for you and says, "Come, sit for a little. We're just trying to solve all the problems of the world together."

This scene is exactly how the Christian Education MindShift got its start. An informal group of Christian educators, composed of multiple school and organizational leaders, found themselves convening several times over the course of a year on hotel patios. We all shared a deep love for and commitment to Christian education, but also felt a common dissatisfaction with the resistance to change, entrenched and ineffective practice, and malaise toward innovation that we observed in Christian education as a whole. After multiple times burning the midnight oil on these issues, we looked at each other squarely and soberly, and asked the scariest and most dangerous question any group can ask of itself: "So, what are we going to do about it?"

By no means were we the first group of Christian educators

to ask this question. In fact, we spent a lot of time talking about our mentors and friends who were forerunners in educational change, people we admired and knew personally. We expressed our gratitude for how they moved us forward as individuals and as a field writ large, encouraging us toward greater faithfulness to Jesus and effectiveness as educators. And yet, we were also aware that the challenges facing Christian school teachers and leaders are not just "new"—they are more complex and disruptive than anything we've encountered before. Beyond technical solutions, we needed an entirely new way of thinking about these challenges. We needed a way to catalyze change in Christian education.

The challenges facing Christian school teachers and leaders are not just "new"—they are more complex and disruptive than anything we've encountered before. Beyond technical solutions, we needed an entirely new way of thinking about these challenges.

Through our individual work in education, a few of us had come in contact with Rex Miller, a well-regarded futurist. Rex is the creator of the MindShift process, a method for envisioning transformational change, which he has facilitated in multiple industries and fields, including education.[1] We began to talk with Rex about doing a MindShift in *Christian* education. A committed believer, he was eager to help us get started and walk with us through the process. For the next two years, a group of about 60 educational leaders—including teachers, heads of school, researchers, entrepreneurs, technologists, practical theologians, attorneys, and others—journeyed together through a series of MindShift dialogues.[2]

1. Rex Miller, "Become a Market Leader by Solving Wicked Problems," accessed May 20, 2019, http://rexmiller.com/mindshift/.

2. Generous support for the Christian Education MindShift was provided by the Christian Education Charitable Trust (CECT) of the Maclellan Foundation, the Association of Christian Schools International (ACSI), the Center for the Advancement of Christian Education (CACE), and the Christian Coalition of Educational Innovation (CCEI).

We will outline the MindShift process shortly, but before we do, we lay out in greater detail the rationale for a Christian Education MindShift. In other words, we wish to recapture and summarize the conversations that launched us into this two-year journey together—with the intent of bringing you along as a reader and colleague. MindShift begins with the tension between what we love about Christian education—its story of hope, told through its impact on students and our communities—and the reality that Christian schools are not always fulfilling their potential, all the more so as they stare down a number of serious challenges to their missions and very existence.

The Impact of Christian Education[3]

Does Christian schooling make a difference? In order to demonstrate the difference Christian schooling makes, most of us reach for stories. We talk about students whose lives bear the fruits of a Christian education. These stories provide a powerful testimony that Christian schooling can make a difference to the world beyond the classroom. In addition to our individual stories as educators and schools, large-scale research in recent years—research that takes seriously the Christian mission of schools—has also provided evidence of Christian education outcomes. Two international research studies have sought to tell the full picture of the outcomes of Christian

---

3. With thanks to Dr. Beth Green for preparing this section on outcomes data for Christian schooling.

schooling: *Mapping the Field*[4] and the *Cardus Education Survey.*[5]

Mapping The Field is a systematic review of the research literature on the impact of Christian schooling. Given that we care a great deal about faith formation and the future of the church, the study asked, is Christian schooling the best place to put our efforts, i.e. does it make a difference? The international evidence gathered supported the claim that students at publicly-funded Church of England schools, Roman Catholic schools,[6] and independent schools with a Christian ethos generally report a more positive attitude towards religion and better spiritual health. There was also evidence that graduates of publicly-funded Christian schools in the U.K. and Australia demonstrated higher academic achievement beyond the differences that can be explained by their prior socioeconomic context.[7]

A second research study, the Cardus Education Survey (CES), has been reporting the outcomes of the Christian and non-religious independent school sectors in the U.S. and Canada, and comparing them to public sector graduate outcomes, since 2011. Every two years, the CES surveys a nationally representative sample of graduates between 25 and 39 years old to measure the impact of Christian schooling on their academic, social, political, religious, and spiritual lives. The CES uses sophisticated statistical controls to screen out socioeconomic factors and isolate school effect, and as such has

4. Elizabeth Green and Trevor Cooling, *Mapping the Field* (London: Theos, 2009).

5. Beth Green, Doug Sikkema, David Sikkink, Sara Skiles, and Ray Pennings, "Cardus Education Survey: Educating to Love your Neighbour: The full picture of Canadian graduates" (Hamilton, Ont.: Cardus, 2016); Ray Pennings, Seel, J., Neven Van Pelt, D., David Sikkink, and Kathryn L. Wiens, "Cardus Education Survey: Do the Motivations for Private Religious Catholic and Protestant Schooling in North America Align with Graduate Outcomes?" (Hamilton, Ont.: Cardus, 2011); Ray Pennings, David Sikkink, Ashley Berner, Christian Smith, Julie Dallavis, and Sara Skiles, "Cardus Education Survey: Private Schools for the Public Good" (Hamilton, Ont.: Cardus, 2014); Ray Pennings, David Sikkink, Deanna Van Pelt, Harro Van Brummelen, and Amy von Heyking, "Cardus Education Survey: A Rising Tide Lifts All Boats" (Hamilton, Ont.: Cardus, 2012).

6. Church of England schools and Roman Catholic schools are publicly funded in the U.K., Australia and in some other jurisdictions worldwide.

7. Green and Cooling, *Mapping the Field*, 9.

become the benchmark for measuring independent school outcomes in North America. Looking at CES data, we can clearly see the impact of Christian education in three thematic areas: *educational attainment and employment*; *citizenship and community-mindedness*; and *religious formation*. [8]

Educational Attainment and Employment

Forthcoming data from the U.S. suggests that if a graduate of a Protestant Evangelical high school goes on to post-secondary education they are more likely to finish their degree than a public school graduate, indicating higher completion rates.[9] However, other academic and work-related differences are not as markedly different between Protestant Evangelical Christian school graduates and public school graduates (i.e. number of years spent in education, attainment of higher degrees, entering STEM fields, earning more, and reporting being in a managerial and professional occupation and/or upper levels of those occupations). CES data has consistently found that Protestant Evangelical school graduates in North America are more likely to work in health, education, and social care related fields and more likely to view their work vocationally than a public school graduate. Taken together, this data has sparked a healthy discussion about the purpose of Christian schooling and the

We should be encouraged by our own accounts and by these research findings that the story of Christian education is one of hope. And it is precisely because of Christian education's current and potential impact on our students and communities that we are concerned with its future.

---

8. The results are summarized only briefly here because CES reports on multiple jurisdictions and to report on all of the data would be beyond the scope of this chapter. This body of work merits closer attention and readers are encouraged to access the reports which are freely available for download on the Cardus website at https://www.cardus.ca/research/education/.

9. Cardus Education Survey (Hamilton, Ont: Cardus, forthcoming).

attitudes towards academic excellence, culture-making, and Christian presence in STEM-related fields.

Citizenship and Community-Mindedness

In Western culture the rise of hyper-individualism, political populism, and social isolation have opened up the public conversation about citizenship education in school, particularly the formation of character and civic engagement. While Christian schools may hold differing assumptions about the relationship between the church, school, and the state, the data does reveal trends in how the Christian school sector prepares graduates for citizenship. Successive CES reports in Canada and the U.S. have absolutely refuted the stereotype that graduates of Christian schools are de facto politically and religiously extremist. With respect to politics, the opposite is true: graduates of Evangelical Protestant schools are less likely to be politically engaged than their public school graduates. We should note that some Christian school leaders see this as a challenge and want to equip their graduates to be of greater influence for the common good in the political sphere.

The CES is careful to define character and civic formation within the broader lens of love of neighbor, and measures giving and volunteering as proxies for the ways that Christian beliefs influence behaviors in the community through and beyond family and religious congregation. Protestant Evangelical school graduates tithe at much higher levels than do public school graduates and more of their volunteering and service seems to be focused through their church communities. Attending a Christian school appears to bolster religious affiliation and connectedness in a culture increasingly in need of hopeful models of community. The data also shows that Christian school graduates are impacted by some of the more challenging stories in our culture; for example, forthcoming U.S. data shows that Protestant Evangelical graduates are more likely to report that culture is hostile to their religious values. However, there are few differences in reported levels of trust in government, media, and science between Christian school graduates and public school graduates in North America. This suggests a hopeful story—

that Christian school graduates may be continuing to be, as James Davidson Hunter terms, "faithfully present"[10] in their communities, despite the hostility toward their Christian faith they may perceive.

Religious Formation

What difference does school sector make to the religious and spiritual lives of graduates? The data consistently points to the influence of Protestant Evangelical schooling above and beyond the religious influence of family and congregation; attending a Protestant Evangelical high school reinforces orthodox Christian beliefs such as belief in a personal God and the infallibility of the Bible. Graduates of Protestant Evangelical schools are more likely to feel obligated to keep spiritual disciplines such as personal prayer and bible study. The most recent U.S. study shows that Protestant Evangelical school graduates attend religious services at much higher rates than public school graduates. These stories from the CES data should offer hope to those who believe that the purpose of Christian schooling is distinctive religious and spiritual formation.

As we read through the above research-demonstrated outcomes of Christian schooling—such as purpose-driven career choices, community-mindedness and increased financial giving and volunteerism, and stronger religious affiliation and practice—we can think of Christian school graduates who exemplify these missional outcomes. In fact, as you read through this summary of the research, most likely students' faces and names came to mind who embody these trends. These are the findings in research and in our own experiences that encourage us that Christian education does, indeed, make a difference.

The Future of Christian Education

We should be encouraged by our own accounts and by these research

---

10. James Davison Hunter, *To Change the World: The Irony, Tragedy, and Possibility of Christianity in the Late Modern World* (Oxford: Oxford University Press, 2010).

findings that the story of Christian education is one of hope. And it is precisely because of Christian education's current and potential impact on our students and communities that we are concerned with its future.

As mentioned earlier, Christian education faces a host of contemporary challenges. Christian schools in Western nations are facing significant threats to sustainability and relevance. Certainly, an increasingly secular Western culture—accompanied by cultural shifts in areas like morality, the family, and even views of truth and reality—is at play. The resultant changing faith profile of parents, in which the number of self-identified Christians is shrinking (particularly among Millennials), presents a challenge to Christian school enrollments.[11] A more competitive educational marketplace is also contributing to this trend, where parents are presented with a proliferation of school options like public charter schools and online academies.

The challenges we face can be reframed as opportunities to provide an education that is more authentically Christian—that better engages today's students in their learning, that helps students to move more deeply into a connection and relationship with God, and that equips students to actively participate in Jesus' redemptive work.

These are challenges that are largely outside of the Christian school's control. However, we also have not done well in addressing challenges that are inside our control, such as responding proactively to rapid technological innovation, diversification of schools, changing learners' needs, and shifts in family structure. Regarding education as a whole, Miller, Latham, and Cahill (2017) assert "the current system is failing to graduate students who are prepared for the demands of

11. Barna Group and Association of Christian Schools International, *Multiple Choice: How Parents Sort Education Options in a Changing Market* (Colorado Springs, CO: ACSI; Ventura, CA: Barna Group, 2017).

the twenty-first century."[12] Christian education is not immune to this reality and the structural challenges that contribute to it. Moreover, compared to other sectors of education, Christian schools overall have been slow to identify and implement innovative and research-based practices—and in some cases, are skeptical of such practices specifically, and educational research generally.[13]

The confluence of both external and internal challenges has resulted in a "perfect storm of discontent, dysfunction and disengagement in our traditional system of education"[14] including a majority of Christian schools. Many of today's Christian school teachers are opening their instructional toolboxes, only to find they lack the tools needed to engage today's hyper-connected—yet overly anxious and isolated—students.[15] Likewise, Christian school leaders are searching for more adequate approaches that lead to measurable student outcomes and return on investment for families, while doing far more with less in a new market reality. This has led Christian educators to ask important questions, such as:

- What is distinctive about Christian education? Why should parents choose Christian schools, for example, over and above maintaining a biblically faithful presence in public education or independent schools with specialized curricula or reputations for academic rigor?
- What should teaching and learning look like in contemporary society, as today's educators and students serve God's purpose in their own generation (Acts 13:36)?
- What knowledge and skills do today's students need in

---

12. Rex Miller, Bill Latham, and Brian Cahill, *Humanizing the Education Machine: How to Create Schools that Turn Disengaged Kids into Inspired Learners* (Hoboken, NJ: John Wiley & Sons, Inc., 2017), 4.

13. Lynn Swaner, *Professional Development for Christian School Educators and Leaders: Frameworks and Best Practices* (Colorado Springs, CO: ACSI, 2016), 21.

14. Miller, Latham, and Cahill, *Humanizing the Education Machine*, 4.

15. For a discussion of trends among today's students, see Jean M. Twenge's book, *iGen: Why Today's Super-Connected Kids Are Growing Up Less Rebellious, More Tolerant, Less Happy—and Completely Unprepared for Adulthood—and What That Means for the Rest of Us* (New York: Atria Books, 2017).

order to be salt and light in an increasingly secular, globally-interdependent, and rapidly changing society and workplace?

- What should Christian schools look like (both programmatically and physically), given the exponential growth of online, on-demand, and personalized learning?
- How can Christian schools be relevant and nimble in a competitive marketplace, and what actions must they take today to position themselves for the future? [16]

As disorienting and disequilibrating as it is, the current educational and cultural moment provides a ripe opportunity to reshape Christian education. Andy Wolfe, Deputy Chief Education Officer (Leadership Development) for the Church of England, explains: "The pressure is on—in terms of budget, in terms of accountability, in terms of staffing and retention and recruitment, and all the things that you're demanded to be doing. And when there is pressure on about the *what* of education, then we're much more attracted to the *why* of education."[17]

The challenges we face can be reframed as opportunities to provide an education that is *more authentically* Christian—that better engages today's students in their learning, that helps students to move more deeply into a connection and relationship with God, and that equips students to actively participate in Jesus' redemptive work. These opportunities hold promise for responsive Christian schools to go further in and further out, with the story of hope and love they can tell to their students and to the culture.

Undoubtedly, a vision for the future of Christian education will require new ways of teaching and leading; ultimately, it may transform the fundamental look and feel of classrooms and schools. But such a transformation will be necessary to prepare future generations of students to "live a life worthy of the Lord and please

---

16. Lynn Swaner and JuLee Mecham, "What is the Future of Christian School Education?" *Christian School Education* 21, no.1 (2017): 6-8.

17. Erik Ellefsen, *A Vision for Education from the UK: Conversation with Nigel Genders and Andy Wolfe, Digical Education* (December 12, 2018), accessed May 20, 2019: https://epellefsen.podbean.com/e/a-vision-for-education-from-the-uk-conversation-with-nigel-genders-and-andy-wolfe/.

him in every way; bearing fruit in every good work, growing in the knowledge of God" (Colossians 1:10).

The Change Method of MindShift

It is essential to realize that, despite what we might wish, "There are no silver bullets…*Complex problems are never solved but can only be navigated or reframed.*"[18] Navigating and reframing the complex challenges and opportunities facing our schools will require more than piecemeal, haphazard, or isolated efforts at change. Rather, what is needed is an intentional and robust process for generating adaptive strategies at both the classroom and school levels. A significant need is to develop a common language, which research findings from *Mapping the Field* concluded Christian education practitioners and researchers do not share when it comes to talking about values, character education, spirituality, or ethos.

This book is an invitation to you—both to the MindShift conversation itself, and to spark or deepen the change process in your own classrooms and schools.

For all of these reasons, we became interested in MindShift as a change method. MindShift helps to envision and catalyze transformational change, and as mentioned earlier has already been used in the field of education. The Christian Education MindShift was modeled on this process, which involved gathering upwards of 60 subject matter experts (SMEs) over the course of several months for a series of guided conversations and visits to innovative school sites. The MindShift process involves a series of steps, as follows:[19]

1. **Identify the problem and the participants.** Begin with a

---

18. Miller, Latham, and Cahill, *Humanizing the Education Machine*, 18, emphasis in original.

19. Ibid.

"wicked problem"[20]—one that is industry-wide and intractable. Then identify a cohort of "knowledgeable leaders commonly frustrated by a broken record of failed attempts to untie the knot that preserves entrenched thinking and obsolete ways." These leaders must commit to meeting together long-term, without predetermined answers.

2. **Uncover the root of the problem.** The cohort identifies the root issues behind the problem, including unproductive metanarratives and assumptions. Participants then ask, "So, what's the problem?" and "What keeps the issue stuck and resistant to change?"

3. **Identify those who are innovating to solve the problem.** The group then finds and visits "those who have broken loose, who are breaking the rules with superior results" in order to observe, learn, and ask, "Just how did you overcome the barriers?" and "What price did you pay challenging the established norms?"

4. **Synthesize learning from these innovators.** The group works to "connect the dots and synthesize our lessons into commonly applicable and scalable principles, habits and tools."

5. **Create prototypes.** The group develops prototypes that will "shift out thinking and test the principles and tools."

6. **Translate the learning.** The group works to "distill the lessons—written in accessible marketplace language" for others.

7. **Create a platform.** Finally, a platform is developed for disseminating the MindShift story and "shifting the conversation toward adopting the new possibilities."

The book you now hold is a synthesis of our learning from this process over the past two years, both from each other and from innovative schools we have visited. Each chapter provides the perspective of authors who have been involved with MindShift, as well as case stories of schools that have engaged in their own change process. And you will find the roots of the problem—in other words, the adaptive challenges facing Christian schools—in the chapter

---

20. Miller, "Become a Market Leader," http://rexmiller.com/mindshift/.

titles. From machine to human, scarcity to abundance, isolated to networked, White to mosaic, Gutenberg to 5G, siloed to engaged, and fear to hope—these are all shifts that need to happen in Christian schools' and educators' stories if we are to flourish into the future.

There is still work to be done in catalyzing change. Specifically, we are actively building a network of schools that can engage in their own MindShift process and share their learning in real time. We also are looking to link schools in creating prototypes for innovation, similar to an open-source approach to knowledge building and sharing. In the meantime, this book is an invitation to you—both to the MindShift conversation itself, and to spark or deepen the change process in your own classrooms and schools. To that end, we hope you'll team up with colleagues in reading this book. Authors have provided discussion questions at the end of each chapter to help with reflection and generating conversation.

Without further ado, we invite you to journey with us— together as colleagues and friends—in our unfolding story of the MindShift in Christian education.

Welcome to MindShift

Rex Miller

Nearly fifty years ago, Alvin Toffler saw that the pace of change was racing faster than individual psyches and society could digest. He also predicted "massive adaptational breakdown" for those who did not acclimate to the new world.[1] The church and Christian education are not exempt from this pace of change. Thirty years later, Loren Mead wrote, "All the institutions and patterns of life that grew up during Christendom are having their foundations shaken."[2] The best illustration I can use for this is what a high school principal at a Christian school recently told me. When he asked his students where they go to church on Sundays, almost two-thirds said, "Online."

Both Toffler and Mead, looking out from vastly divergent viewpoints, saw the same thing: the future is coming, and it will not wait for us to approve or adapt. Just as a baby does not have the option of remaining in the warm and comfortable womb when the time for birth arrives, we are all being pushed out of our comfort zones into a world we do not yet know.

My company, MindShift, is built around the idea of catalyzing new, transformative ways of viewing difficult problems. Perhaps the

---

1. Alvin Toffler, *Future Shock* (New York: Random House, 1970).

2. Loren Mead, *The Once and Future Church* (Boulder: Rowman & Littlefield Publishers, 2001).

best description of a MindShift was published by John Newton in 1779: "I was blind, but now I see." A MindShift transports you from a dark world into a brand-new, vibrant, full-color realm of new vision, hope, confidence, creativity, and energy. That kind of life-altering change can come to individuals, families, churches, companies, and even nations.

Wicked Problems

Engaging in transformative thinking, like in our MindShifts, is becoming necessary in today's world, because we are confronting more and more challenges that are now commonly called "wicked problems." In this usage, wicked does not denote evil. Rather, it identifies problems that are very difficult, even impossible, to solve. Such problems actually resist solutions, whether due to incomplete or conflicting information about the problem, a large number of people or stakeholders involved, or the interlocked nature of the problem.

Schools are asking our teachers to prepare kids for a world that no longer exists.

Consider the problems we face today: health care; terrorism; climate change; human trafficking. The complexity, conflicting information, lack of consensus, and interconnectedness with other problems renders them unsolvable. Most attempts to solve these kinds of problems become nothing more than a complicated game of "Whack-a-Mole": when you hit one aspect of the problem, another one pops up. Therefore, rather than solving or eradicating the problem, you end up dancing with it.

We know we likely have a wicked problem on our hands if any of the following is true:

- the problem won't go away;
- everyone is equally frustrated for different reasons;
- the whole industry seems stuck;
- no one can solve it on their own;
- the problem leads to finger pointing;

- we've adapted as an industry to accept sub-par performance; and
- margins decline while costs increase.

Take a minute and read that list again. Does anything strike you as familiar in your context? Yes, or not really? What if we reframed this list in educational language, and asked instead:

- Has your school enrollment dropped, while your tuition and costs have increased?
- Is your financial model for your school looking unsustainable over the long term, but there are no ready answers for how to fix it?
- Are your students engaging fully in their learning so they are thriving and succeeding at their maximum potential, or have you (and they) come to expect less than what they're capable of?
- Is the school leveraging technology in ways that lead to positive outcomes for students, or does it feel like you're all on a technology hamster wheel—spending incalculable money on the latest and greatest, training and retraining staff, and putting usage rule after rule in place, only to feel like student learning isn't improving?
- Are your leaders, teachers, and/or students approaching the point of burnout?
- Do your parents point fingers at the school (and vice versa), instead of working collaboratively toward student success?

Over the past few years, I've joined teams of stakeholders to tackle wicked problems related to commercial real estate, workplace wellness, and yes, education. In our MindShift in education we had over 60 subject matter experts, from diverse fields and backgrounds, journey together for a year and a half as we dialogued together and visited schools that were successful outliers—meaning these schools defied all the odds in becoming places where kids and educators thrived.

The book *Humanizing the Education Machine: How to Create Schools that Turn Disengaged Kids into Inspired Learners*[3] was the result of that MindShift process. What follows in this chapter is a discussion of the findings of our education MindShift, followed by reflections on what is common as well as unique to Christian schools—and what Christian education needs for a MindShift to happen.

Forces that Necessitate a MindShift[4]

In the middle of the 15th century, Johannes Gutenberg converted a mechanical wine press into a printing press. That was more than an invention; it launched a revolution, a continental divide of history that marked the end of oral culture and established the power and dominance of the printed word. History had never witnessed such an explosion of innovation in art, science, religion, exploration, commerce education and that period's crowning achievement—the nation-state, a government formed on an idea and constituted by commonly held principles.

That seminal event influenced—and continues to shape—everything within education. The print era led to systems designed for standardization and conformity. It therefore brought about common language, common understanding, common purpose, and common standards. It allowed a new level of coordination and cooperation never before possible, and it did so marvelously well.

Education before the 21st century provided a perfectly designed system for preparing people to function and excel in a Gutenberg world. And that still marks much of education today (including in Christian schools). Sadly, that means many schools are asking our teachers to prepare kids for a world that no longer exists. Our colleges are among the best in the world, which means we train teachers well. We're simply training them to provide the best 20th-century education possible.

---

3. Rex Miller, Bill Latham, and Brian Cahill, *Humanizing the Education Machine: How to Create Schools that Turn Disengaged Kids into Inspired Learners* (Hoboken, NJ: Wiley & Sons, 2017).

4. Portions of this section originated in my book, *Humanizing the Education Machine* (Hoboken, NJ: Wiley & Sons, 2017).

If you're over 50, you have probably asked your child or grandchild to set up a smartphone or connect the Wi-Fi. The kids, of course, did it quickly and without any need for instructions. Those kids are digital natives (generally understood to be those born after 1998). They are the first generation in history that understands more about how the new world really works than those who are still "in charge." A revolution is coming: 70 million digital natives will be rewriting the world based on their worldview and skills. The rest of us will soon be left behind.

The implications for education are profound and long-term, and they challenge all the rules and assumptions of traditional schools. We can illustrate this by way of an example in real life. Our MindShift worked with a K-12 school in Florida whose principal asked students to write essays on what they thought 21st century learning could look like and how they best learn. The students poured out garden-fresh ideas: they thought the teacher should not be in the front of the class. They wanted learning to be more hands-on, team-based, and peer-driven. They wanted to sit in comfortable and rolling chairs. And, why not have round tables with built-in-computers? Those responses led to a larger conversation in the school, which led to bringing in a graphic designer to illustrate those ideas for the school's director of construction. And he created cardboard mockups of furniture, technologies, wall writing surfaces, and other details as designed by the kids and teachers. Then a local architect took the ideas and developed a concept plan, along with a budget for converting classrooms into what students would need in the future.

The classroom of the future treats students humanely—as humans gifted with talents, abilities, and agency. Yes, the classroom of the future needs to integrate technology. But more importantly, it needs to be built on a human—not a machine—scale.

Let me ask you again to pause, and then re-read the story above. When you read it, what did you see, and what did you focus on? Your answer to these questions is important. Was it the use of technology? Was it the redesign of physical space, furniture, and so forth, to create the classroom of the future? If that's what you noticed in this story, you wouldn't be wrong. But you also wouldn't be entirely right.

What really transformed this classroom toward future-readiness was the empowerment of students to share their views and stories and to think creatively—and our taking them seriously in shaping the learning environment that, after all, is supposed to be geared toward them and their learning. In other words, the classroom of the future treats students humanely—as humans gifted with talents, abilities, and agency. Yes, the classroom of the future needs to integrate technology. But more importantly, it needs to be built on a human—not a machine—scale.

When Christian education focuses more on students acquiring static knowledge than developing a rich context for life-long learning, it misses opportunities for authentic growth, discipleship, mentoring, and application in real life.

What do I mean by machine? By design, institutions can deliver services, but they cannot care. Individuals within those institutions—like doctors, nurses, and teachers—can certainly demonstrate care for those they serve. But the need for efficiency and accountability necessarily constrains the caring impulses. The need for efficiency and collective strength pushes certain activities and dynamics "up" into larger, corporate, even governmental structures. These include places like hospitals and schools. Those same doctors and nurses and teachers are always under pressure to help greater numbers, manage a larger caseload, complete more paperwork, and master ever-changing procedures and policies. At some point, everything and everyone in the institution gets forced into bureaucratic behavior.

The public education machine has not changed very much over the century or so since it was invented to provide widescale, standardized preparation for industrial-age workers. It's only good (and even then, marginally so) with batches—cramming kids into arbitrary age groups, and doing its business on an arbitrary calendar schedule. It's a factory system. In my family's experience, my wife and I put three of our kids into that factory many years ago. And when they couldn't conform to the dominant model and expectations for standardized and one-size-fits-all learning, the machine chewed up two of them. I'm sorry to share that when we moved our second one to a Christian school, she got chewed up there, too. When our third child began showing the same signs of distress and disengagement in middle school, we decided not to let the machine have its way again; instead, we home-schooled him after the age of 12.

In our personal and my professional experience, the Christian school machine has some similarities to public education's machine. But it also falls prey to certain mentalities that raise themselves up against the knowledge of God (2 Corinthians 10:5). For example, many Christian schools have been pressed into a bunker mentality; the machine insists that the students be protected from the world. By doing so, they miss a vast and historic opportunity to prepare kids with the confidence to move through—and change—the world! And when Christian education focuses more on students acquiring static knowledge than developing a rich context for life-long learning, it misses opportunities for authentic growth, discipleship, mentoring, and application in real life. In other words, student outcomes become limited to how well students "hear" what they learn, versus putting what they learn into action as "doers" of God's word (James 1:22).

All of that is part of the education machine's legacy. And the machine has no answers when it comes to the pressing questions we need to ask, such as:

1. OK, folks, what century do we live in?
2. How can we best prepare the students for what lies ahead?
3. How can we help students develop a redemptive attitude toward "the world"?
4. How do we provide real experiences that prepare students to be Christ's agents of reconciliation?

And that's why we need a MindShift.

Christian Education at the Crossroads[5]

In its infancy, the church faced an enormous adaptive problem: its message and mission were much more extensive than anyone had ever seen or dared to imagine. It was too big to just stay in Jerusalem, so challenges (read: persecution) forced it to spread out and begin pouring into a world that most believers of that time considered alien and toxic.

If we think about Christian schools in the same way, we begin to engage in the MindShift. The gospel-based hope undergirding Christian education is too powerful to be trapped in standardized, machine-like institutions. So we need to reframe the challenges that Christian schools face right now as opportunities, which can drive teachers and schools to take new risks and pour out into their communities via an education that has been "humanized" by God.

Let me suggest five areas where the MindShift needs to be triggered:

1. **Isolation.** Many churches and Christian schools remain isolated from the realities of their larger communities. Many are caught in what one leader described to me as "the fear of contamination." But the only way to overcome isolation is to develop social capital—the tapestry of relationships, values, behavior, and cultural assets that empower cooperation in any communal group. That cannot be done without becoming more engaged with the larger community.

2. **Fragmentation.** Too many churches and Christian schools are so fragmented and activity-driven that they have little opportunity to develop strong relational bonds among faculty, staff, leaders, and students. And that creates an unhealthy "churn rate." That business term refers to the number of people who enter, leave, or change roles within an organization. Schools, including Christian schools, are not exempt from this phenomenon. Obviously, a high churn rate damages the

---

5. Portions of this section originated in my book, *The Millennium Matrix* (San Francisco: Jossey-Bass, 2004).

cohesiveness of the organization, not to mention the well-being of individuals. (My next MindShift project looks at the root causes, such as stress and the caregiver's burden, that lead to incredibly high burnout rates for educators.)

3. Lack of Identity. Fragmentation often arises as a symptom of lack of identity. That deficiency cannot be reversed by being "purpose-driven" or having a great mission statement. The school's identity is found in its belonging to Christ, which grows fuller through steadily spending time together in meaningful fellowship and service as a community of believers.

4. Central Leadership. The industrial-age centrality of leadership, as exercised via command and control, can prevent adaptation and innovation. Too many church and educational entities maintain a constricting leash on what they approve. They operate like a central command post, when a more decentralized and federation form of governance might be more blessed and more beneficial.

We need to reframe the challenges that Christian schools face right now as opportunities, which can drive teachers and schools to take new risks and pour out into their communities via an education that has been "humanized" by God.

5. Lack of Innovation. Likely related to their leadership structure, many churches and Christian schools can be described as "sclerotic," or rigid and inflexible. They do not tolerate outlier or even unusual elements. But that constraint of human creativity opposes the very nature of a creative God. So many biblical stories reveal the unruly, uncontrollable, and unconventional initiatives that spring from God's Spirit hovering over people. Godly leaders know to not box God—or the people of God—in.

Telling the Story

In thinking through areas that require a MindShift, I encourage people to communicate them through stories. Most of us are generally defensive when it comes to change, but telling stories helps to avoid the creation of walls of resistance. Stories can suggest a new reality and even demonstrate vulnerability. Donald Miller says, "Nobody can look away from a good story."[6] That is why MindShift is more about harnessing the power of the story than laying out proposals or arguments.

"The Hero's Journey" (as told by Joseph Campbell and others) is considered the classic pattern behind every Hollywood story. The hero has to simultaneously journey away "from" something old and "to" something new (usually the "something" is a way of thinking, being, or doing). Think of *Raiders of the Lost Ark, Harry Potter, Up, The Lion King,* or pretty much any of your favorite movies, and you'll find the hero's journey carrying the plot.

Believers are continually on the path from redemption to renewal. That is God's "from…to" story in our lives—and Jesus is our hero, who leads out in front.

According to screenwriter Christopher Vogler, "Stories built on the model of the Hero's Journey have an appeal that can be felt by everyone, because they well up from a universal source in the shared unconscious and reflect universal concerns."[7] Christians know better, because we know the universal source: we are all part of a larger story, which is the narrative arc of the Bible. Believers are continually on the path from redemption to renewal. That is God's "from…to" story in our lives—and Jesus is our hero, who leads out in front.

Throughout this book, the specific "from…to" stories that a Christian Education MindShift must tell are reflected in the chapter

---

6. Donald Miller, *Building a Story Brand* (Harper Collins, 2017).

7. Christopher Vogler, *The Writer's Journey* (Michael Wiese Productions, 1992).

titles. As you follow the stories, they can help you imagine what a MindShift would look like in your own setting. And because this is a book written by and for Christian educators, you will find Jesus front and center in those stories—just as He wants to be in yours.

One final note: just because we are on a "from...to" journey doesn't mean we know exactly where we are headed. As people who walk in Christian faith, our whole life should unfurl in a grand adventure of exploration. After all, the Bible tells us something about the grand patriarch of faith: "By faith, Abraham...went out, not knowing where he was going" (Hebrews 11:8). We have many more heroes of the faith (Hebrews 11) who responded to God's call without seeing clearly but still trusting Him. In the same way, we too are moving beyond what we know.

The Christian Education MindShift begins by recognizing this is a good thing—and probably even a "God thing." As people of faith, we can never get too comfortable with where we are, and we can never really control where we are going—after all, we walk by faith and not by sight. Ultimately, a MindShift doesn't just help us move into new and scary unknowns. It also helps us renew our minds (Romans 12:2) and, by moving us out of our comfort zones, love and serve our neighbors who live in the regions beyond.

From Machine to Human

Dan Beerens, Justin Cook, and Katie Wiens

Picture a machine in your mind. The machine could be simple, like the Rube Goldberg ones our students make. Or, you might picture a complex machine, comprised of multiple smaller machines, like an automobile assembly line or those found in a food processing and packaging plant. As you visualize your machine, consider this: what goes into the machine, what happens to it, and what does it look like when it comes out?

Regardless of which machine you visualize, all machines have certain features in common. For example, they control for common inputs, by selecting which materials go into the machine. They use standardized and sequenced processes to act forcefully on those inputs. And ultimately, their goal is to produce homogeneous products (think widgets). If for some reason a specific outcome of their process looks different from what was intended, it is deemed defective—and is at risk of being discarded.

It doesn't take much further imagination to see today's modern educational system as machine-like in its essence. We group students by age, force them through a year-by-year standardized course of study, and assess their progress using a one-size-fits all set of standardized tests. Much of what happens to them in classrooms is exactly that—the teaching and curriculum happens *to* them, as they are unidirectionally taught content, with the expectation that they will retain and demonstrate mastery of it. And of course we know what happens to students who don't succeed in "making the grade." At best, they're provided with extensive support to help them get back to the spot on the conveyor belt where they belong, and at worst, they're either forced off entirely after repeated "failure"—or become so discouraged they decide to drop out on their own. We borrow a term from Rex Miller and others in referring to this superstructure of Western schooling as "the education machine," which is designed to produce a uniform outcome with efficiency being the primary goal.

Machines work well for the industrial purposes for which they were invented. We contend they do not, however, work well in forming human beings, who are created in the image of God (Genesis 1:26)—and as such are fearfully and wonderfully made (Psalm 139:14), diverse in their backgrounds and contexts (Acts 17:26), and uniquely gifted for good works as part of God's redemptive plan (Ephesians 2:10). So how did we end up with an educational system that is so far afield from God's design for human flourishing, and how can Christian schools move closer to a vision of education that is commensurate with that design?

A Brief History of the Education Machine

Education is never neutral. We are often reminded of this reality as we consider our distinctiveness as Christian schools. In 1635 Boston Latin School was among the first organized public schools, founded to ensure the Puritan elite of Boston developed strong Biblical literacy and were held to the highest of academic standards. Schoolmasters were hired to achieve that aim, and the time spent in the study of Latin, classic literature, and religion dominated the school day.

This model proliferated through the colonies for a century and perpetuated the religious, social, and academic stratification in the early years of the Union. In 1837, Horace Mann, also a member of the Boston elite, would take the position of the Secretary of the Massachusetts Board of Education and conceptualize a new vision of public education, the common school. In Mann's view, education would be a norming force that would level the social order of the day most efficiently, as he believed that children were indeed the most malleable of society. The common school aimed to redeem some of the social ills of the time by ensuring robust civic engagement, allaying class conflict, and accomplishing a host of other social aims by instilling moral habits based upon a Universalist religious doctrine.

In the common school movement, arguably the most powerful influence on education in the United States and perhaps North America, social harmony was the highest value, and therefore the structure of the school—from the curriculum to the teaching—prioritized a uniformity of thought and behavior. Students learned to read using Noah Webster's Blue Backed Speller and later the McGuffey Readers, each of which intended to teach moral behavior while students learned to read increasingly difficult texts. As the value of the schools moved from prioritizing Calvinist theology to Universalist theology, so too did the excerpts in the readers. While this movement can clearly take credit for catalyzing a more educated populace—literacy rates skyrocketed for instance—some would argue the approach had a cost.

How did we end up with an educational system that is so far afield from God's design for human flourishing, and how can Christian schools move closer to a vision of education that is commensurate with that design?

Primarily, and most relevant to this chapter, many believe this movement stifled creative thought and individual growth, instead prioritizing uniform outcomes achieved most efficiently for the taxpayer, a utilitarian legacy that schools—both public and private—have inherited. In the view of one historian, "the American public school is a gigantic standardized compromise most of us have learned to live with,"[1] a sentiment that we would argue persists still today across North America in public and private schools alike.

As with any machine, choices are made in the design to enable a particular product to be made, like the widgets imagined at the

---

1. Carl Kaestle, "Conflict and Consensus Revisited: Notes toward a Reinterpretation of American Educational History," *Harvard Educational Review 46, no. 3* (August 1976): 396.

outset of this chapter. In the case of the education machine, the desired product was a uniform populace, and therefore decisions about the design of that machine, such as the schedule of the day, age grouping, and teaching methods, for example, were made to achieve that end. Perhaps most significantly, the driving purpose of the education machine is the transactional nature of students producing work so that a teacher can "grade" it. In turn, this led to the entire system relying on standardization in order to measure its effectiveness and efficiently allocate resources. While the aims of schools have most certainly evolved, we are left with the structures of the education machine—and we believe many of those structures are making it difficult, if not impossible, to achieve the aims of today's Christian school.

We are left with the structures of the education machine—and we believe many of those structures are making it difficult, if not impossible, to achieve the aims of today's Christian school.

Telling A Different Story

If the education machine looks at students through the eyes of efficiency and utility and transaction, by contrast a humane education rooted in the Christ story looks at students through the eyes of love. The Christ story comes from the life and person of Jesus Christ, the second person of the Trinity—the center of the universe, the one, as we are told in Colossians, in whom all things cohere and hold together, the source of all love, beauty, truth, and goodness:

Truth is a network of relationships; any one person, thing or event stands at the intersection of a vast number of these. Ultimately, truth is the *relationality* that is God's covenant community, held at the centre by the cosmic Christ. Not reason but love is at the heart of Creation. All God's creatures are made in relationships of service with one another. It is an interdependent creation in which meaning lies not in things in and of themselves but in their connections with one another.[2]

The Christ story flowing from this love and interdependence tells of the value of each person as unique in all creation and as bearing the image of God. It tells a larger story of a citizenship in another kingdom, a compelling and beautiful vision of a new land where the inhabitants are free from the perniciousness of sin, division, hatred, brokenness, evil, and all things opposed to human wholeness and flourishing. The Christ story suggests that the achievement of this vision of wholeness, beauty and flourishing can begin right now.

As humans we periodically experience glimpses of this wholeness through the avenues of beauty, truth and goodness, a feeling that something is "just right," and as Christ followers we hunger for more. This hunger for a more complete life of wholeness and harmony with God, nature, neighbor, and self leads us to reject philosophy, pedagogy, and practices that are transactional and dehumanizing and to seek ways of teaching and learning that better reflect a God-focused, image-bearer flourishing approach. This desire flows from a rejection of the concept of the self-made man as the measure of all things and a recognition of the sovereignty of God and our ultimate purpose as human beings to worship him and offer our lives in service to his kingdom.

Schools that focus on understanding and emulating the character of Christ seek to teach students what it might mean to be like Christ in contemporary society. What might it look like to be reshaped into a Christ follower—a true disciple seeking first how best to love neighbor and the world and to not seek first one's own agenda and advancement? This seeking to be a Christ follower, done well, should put students at odds with the stories of success and self-aggrandizement put forth by peers, family, cultural icons, and a world that rejects the Christ story. It should also put educators at odds with the default transactional nature of education as grade acquisition for personal gain. The Christ story starts by offering a fundamental re-orientation of the purpose of education—from adoration of man

---

2. Doug Blomberg, "Whose Spirituality? Whose Rationality? A Narrational Locus for Learning," *Journal of Education and Christian Belief* 13, no. 2 (2009): 118.

and his achievements, toward the worship of God and his desire for human flourishing as expressed through the life and work of Jesus Christ. To help students to flourish means we are not simply focused on academics or the spiritual—we seek to show students a holistic approach to all of life, not just life at school.

Schools seeking to implement the Christ story of love will ultimately be measured by the desire expressed by their students to practice the faith that they see modeled by the life work and love of Jesus Christ and lived out by adults in their lives. Our key measure of success is whether students connect to the Christ story of love in personal ways that motivate and direct them into a life that lives out this story. If we hope for this kind of result then all aspects of our current models of educating students in Christian schools involving philosophy, pedagogy, and practices should be examined rigorously to see if they are in the end helping students to: 1) better understand the ultimate purposes of life; 2) become more Christ-like, as enactors of the shalom of God; and 3) live into the Christ story of love throughout their entire lives—to learn "to live the alternative reality of the kingdom of God within the present world order faithfully."[3]

This leads us to the question of what kind of changes will it take to implement the Christ story more effectively in our current models. However, because most of today's educators grew up inside the education machine and were professionally trained to sustain and replicate it in our schools, it is extremely difficult to envision the necessary changes in the abstract. By way of popular metaphor, the fish that lives its whole life in a fish tank has no knowledge of the ocean.

In order to overcome these limitations, we need to consider schools that are actively living out Christ's story of love in practice. We devote the remainder of this chapter to one such school.

The Story in Action

Located just outside the massive urban sprawl of the greater Toronto

---

3. James Davison Hunter, *To Change the World: The Irony, Tragedy, and Possibility of Christianity in the Late Modern World*, (Oxford: Oxford University Press, 2010), 236.

area, Halton Hills Christian School (HHCS) is a school on a journey.

Principal Marianne Vangoor knew that she and her staff were passionately committed to the well-being of the 350 PreK-8 students in the school, but she believed they could do more. As this chapter highlights, Marianne was not content with the status quo of a transactional education of grade acquisition. So she and her staff asked each other a pivotal question at the summer staff retreat in 2015: "What does love require?" This became the staff theme for that year and has shaped the learning journey at HHCS ever since.

The goal for the staff at HHCS in 2018-2019 sums up this desire well: *To be an outpost of grace for families and students alike where young minds and bodies and hearts are nurtured, shaped, taught, and challenged, in order to become active and passionate ambassadors of the King right now and for all of their tomorrows!* [4]

The Christ story starts by offering a fundamental re-orientation of the purpose of education—from adoration of man and his achievements, toward the worship of God and his desire for human flourishing as expressed through the life and work of Jesus Christ.

The goal highlights two key facets of how learning at Halton Hills Christian School moves from machine to human. First, the school is passionate about supporting students inwardly: the development of the whole child in a culture of unconditional love and grace ("young minds *and bodies and hearts* are nurtured, shaped, taught and challenged"). Second, the school is convinced that through their learning, students can actively contribute culturally to the flourishing of others and our world, both near and far ("in order to become active and passionate ambassadors of the King right now and for all of their tomorrows!") This inward and outward formation forms the humanizing learning vision at Halton Hills Christian School.

---

4. Halton Hills Christian School internal document, used with permission.

Inward Formation

HHCS educators believe strongly that social-emotional learning cannot be separated from academic learning, and the school has chosen to use resources from Responsive Classroom to enact this belief. Responsive Classroom is an evidence-based approach that seeks to create a culture of joy and belonging for students, by integrating academic and social-emotional learning.

The daily schedule at HHCS intentionally makes time for this connection of academic success and social-emotional learning. The morning begins with time for devotions in a morning meeting. In developmentally appropriate ways—the meeting looks different in kindergarten from eighth grade—each student starts the day with four key elements:

- A **greeting**, where each child is welcomed and welcomes each other by name;
- A time of **sharing**, where each child has a chance to connect their own stories with the stories of their classmates, recognizing that they all have ways in which they are similar but also ways in which they're different;
- An **activity**, which helps build community and energize their minds and bodies for a day of learning together; and
- A morning **message** from the teacher that gives an indication of passion and purpose for the day.

Each day also provides ten minutes of quiet time after the second nutritional break, so that students can again relax, recharge (especially those more introverted), and re-focus for learning after an outdoor recess. And lastly, the day ends with a closing circle in each classroom, where students have a moment to reflect on the good and the hard parts of their day together before returning home. These practices help to ensure that each student at HHCS is known, loved, and valued as a contributor to school life.

Outward Formation

HHCS is not only committed to supporting students in their inward social/emotional and academic development. At HHCS, a project-based learning (PBL) pedagogy is the key driver of this desire to develop active and passionate ambassadors. Over the past number of years, students have engaged in significant learning projects that have blessed their larger community:

- Preschool students grew their own food in a garden that was planned and maintained by them.
- Kindergarten students became marine biologists, challenged the school community regarding how plastic bottles and bags were used, and then led the way by designing and selling metal water bottles to fund ocean clean up.
- First grade students created HHCS welcome guidebooks for visitors and prospective parents.
- Second and third grade students educated the community about endangered species in the area, by creating an information-packed 18-month calendar.
- Third grade students created an architectural guide for historic buildings in the town of Georgetown to be used by visitors to the town.
- Fourth grade students wrote and illustrated a picture book comparing their daily lives with that of a fourth-grade student in Afghanistan. The sale of the book raised funds to send 200 girls to school in Afghanistan through the non-profit Pennies for Peace.
- Fifth grade students hosted an agricultural fair for the school community that included food trucks, animals, and even a tractor pull.
- Sixth grade students developed an action research project to determine whether or not the main artery Trafalgar Road should be widened, and presented the findings to Halton city planners.
- Seventh and eighth grade students provided leadership for the community to more deeply understand and begin the process of reconciliation with indigenous friends and neighbors.

Student feedback from these projects demonstrates the power of PBL in outward formation. In one of these projects, fifth and sixth grade students published a book of historical fiction, called *From Chains to Freedom*, using the novel *Underground to Canada* as their mentor text. Each student's story was included in the book (not just a handful of the "best"), and the students used the profits of the book sales to support the International Justice Mission Canada in combating modern day slavery. At a school-wide celebration of learning that included this project, one of the students shared how the project helped him to overcome his struggle with editing, as well as how to develop his voice as a writer. In reflecting about what he learned through sharing and selling their book at a local mall, the student commented that "people need to be informed about slavery today. You need to get out of your comfort zone, not stand behind a table and wait for the money." Another student indicated that she was nervous to share her book with others "because we're reading excerpts of our writing in front of an audience. But I'm also pretty excited." Why? "Because I'm really changing history and I'm freeing slaves today in different developing countries."[5]

Christian schools must identify where they have been shaped by cultural forces—such as the industrial-era impulse to construe schools as machines—and instead return to an education founded on God's love for humanity and creation.

In addition to projects like these, each eighth grade student also prepares a graduate presentation to a panel of staff and parents. The presentations are not about grades but about growth. They include a portfolio of the beautiful work the student has created, but more importantly, students reflect on their character formation over the course of their HHCS career. Their presentations address developmental questions such as, How have they grown in their sense of self and in practicing and living out their faith? Where do they see their lives going after HHCS? What is God

---

5. From Student interviews conducted by the authors on March 6, 2019.

calling them into, and how will they serve in the bigger Kingdom?

Supporting the Story

This desire to support students in both their inward formation and their outward cultural contributions through their learning "as ambassadors of the King" takes time and commitment at all levels. For instance, HHCS hires with this vision in mind, recognizing that it is the passionate commitment of teachers that makes this vision for learning a reality. HHCS has also created a position on staff for one of their teachers to be a PBL coach, offering support and expertise to her colleagues. In addition to internal professional learning, many HHCS teachers have attended the Christian Teacher Academy, which is a week-long project design academy with a distinctively Christian model of PBL hosted in the summer in Ontario to support the design of projects like the ones described above. This unique academy helps faculty to address three dimensions of student learning—culture and character; mastery of knowledge and skills; and beautiful work— that emanate from the "core aspects of a Christian school's identity," namely that "Christian schools confess that the life of Jesus Christ is the embodiment of wisdom. Our own lives, and indeed all of creation, are redeemed and restored through him."[6]

HHCS is committed to embodying a growth mindset where beautiful work is created through healthy cultures of critique and revision. Fundamentally, a growth mindset fostered in a culture of love and acceptance requires grace and commitment. To this end, at HHCS students learn how to work together in groups, as well as how to employ conflict resolution techniques and give descriptive feedback that is kind, helpful, and specific. Students track their own learning and growth in their data notebooks and set goals for how they wish to continue to develop.

Faculty themselves are on a similar journey; along with administrators, they have engaged in the "learning walk protocol" where small teams visit all classrooms to look for specific practices

---

6. Christian Teacher Academy, "What is Project Based Learning?" (2015), accessed April 4, 2019, http://www.teacheracademy.ca/academy-model.html.

that have been named as a priority by the full staff. Although the intent is not to judge or evaluate teachers, the teams utilize an observation protocol that lists out items to look for as well as questions to ask students. The data collected is shared and celebrated with the full staff in a letter written by the walkers. The staff has reported that leading with love as educators is hard work, but that the practices highlighted through the learning walk do indeed lead to deep engagement and a sense of purpose for both students and teachers.

A commitment to growth mindset also undergirds the HHCS desire to go deeper in implementing their vision for dynamic learning. Joined by fellow leaders from sister schools in their support organization (Edvance Christian Schools Association), teams from HHCS have visited schools and systems that model the type of learning to which they also aspire (such as A.B. Combs in North Carolina, High Tech High in California, Genesee Community Charter School in New York, and even the Finnish school system). Each visit has provided HHCS teams with an opportunity to both learn how to humanize the education machine from others who are trying to do the same, as well as engage in team learning—which ultimately leads to greater success and fidelity in implementation.

God's Beautiful Story

Although the "education machine" that arose out of the common school movement may have been appropriate for its own time, the Christ story calls into question the inheritance of a system designed for uniformity and efficiency, with grade acquisition as its currency and standardization as its measurement. Our desire to humanize the educational machine is inspired by the Christ story described above. Asking "What does love require?" Halton Hills Christian School offers itself as a school on a journey, hoping to explicitly align its commitments and practices with its stated goal.

In *Beauty Will Save the World: Rediscovering the Allure and Mystery of Christianity,* Brian Zahnd reminds us of one of the mottoes of the Protestant Reformation, "*semper reformanda,*" or the church is always reforming. Zahnd explains that this principle "comes from the realization that there are forces—political, social, theological, spiritual, and so forth—that over time tend to twist the church and the gospel out of shape. As a result the church must continually seek to recover the true form and original beauty found in the gospel of Jesus Christ."[7] Likewise, Christian schools must identify where they have been shaped by cultural forces—such as the industrial-era impulse to construe schools as machines—and instead return to an education founded on God's love for humanity and creation. That is, after all, the more—and the most—beautiful story.

Questions for Discussion

1. How did you experience "the machine" as a student and are you experiencing it now as an educator? Give examples.

2. What are the perceived benefits of the "machine" and why is our education system so driven by it?

3. What are the implications of the Christ story for our teaching, and what elements of the "machine" are competing with the Christ story at your school?

4. If you undertook learning walks in your school to look for values that underpin teaching and decision-making, what might you see?

5. What is most compelling and encouraging to you about the Halton Hills story?

6. What practices or decisions might help your classrooms move away from school as "machine" and more to school as a place designed for human flourishing?

---

7. Brian Zahnd, *Beauty Will Save the World: Rediscovering the Allure and Mystery of Christianity* (Lake Mary, FL: Charisma House, 2012), 3.

From Scarcity to Abundance

Justin Smith and Erik Ellefsen

Educators are the masters of asking questions. Teachers ask students questions all day long, and often encourage students to ask questions in return. Sometimes we even ask students to ask questions of each other. Then administrators ask questions of teachers, and vice versa. We ask a lot of questions in education, because our shared currency in education is knowledge—and questions are a great tool for discovering, trading, and even creating knowledge.

However, not all questions are created equal. There are two types of questions we can ask: *convergent* (close-ended) and *divergent* (open-ended). Convergent questions tend to elicit factual, straightforward responses. For example, we can ask what the formula for the Pythagorean theorem is ($a^2+b^2=c^2$), or whether the Soviet Union is still in existence (no). We can ask whether students had a good night's sleep or understood the homework from last night (most likely no in both cases). Often answers to these types of questions are factual, take little time to conjure, and provide just enough information to move one step further.

Open-ended questions are not as easily answered. They are often wide-ranging, debatable, and drill down to the heart of the matter. However, they tend to result in more nuanced and robust responses. That is why English language arts teachers use open-ended questions for essay prompts in writing classes. For example, we might ask *why* the Soviet Union is no longer in existence, or *how* students approached their homework problems that gave them so much trouble. We also see that in His teaching, Jesus used open-ended questions all the time: "Who do you say I am?" (Matthew 16:15), "Why are you so afraid?" (Mark 4:40), "What do you want me to do for you?" (Mark 10:51). Certainly, Jesus already knew the answers to these questions; as our teacher, He employed them as a way to provoke learning in His listeners and in us.

As the reader, you're probably asking a question of your own right now: Why are these authors spending so much time on different types of questions? The reason is that we believe that only schools that ask good questions can adapt to a rapidly changing world, identify new opportunities, and—in the case of Christian education—live out their missions into the future. Quoting David Hackett Fischer, Warren Berger writes in his book *A More Beautiful Question*, "questions are the engines of intellect."[1] Berger is convinced that innovation and advancement stem from good questions. We are convinced this holds true for educators and schools.

A Matter of Mindset

The types of questions we ask as educators are generally reflective of a larger pattern of thinking, or our *mindset*. And just like questions, our mindset can tend to be close-ended or open-ended.

In education circles, it is fair to assume most professionals are familiar with Carol Dweck's work on mindset.[2] Dweck and her team at Stanford University researched the psychology of success and determined that a person's mindset—either fixed or growth— will determine that person's success with a particular skill or understanding. In a similar way, Angela Duckworth and her team at the University of Pennsylvania studied the effect of a relentless

1. Warren Berger, *A More Beautiful Question: The Power of Inquiry to Spark Breakthrough Ideas* (New York: Bloomsbury, 2014), 15.

2. Carol S. Dweck, *Mindset: The New Psychology of Success* (New York: Ballantine Books, 2008).

resilience, known as *grit*.[3] Dweck's and Duckworth's work intersect in their views that success and failure are largely dependent on people's ability to set their minds to a task, pursue it with determination, and relentlessly believe that practice and work will lead to growth.

We can translate their work directly into the Christian school setting. Christian schools today face a myriad of difficulties related to funding, enrollment, inadequate teachers' salaries, and programmatic quality. These factors can constrain and eventually close schools. Yet we are also aware of many Christian schools that continue to flourish, grow, and empower learners, despite existing with the same difficulties. If both kinds of schools are facing the same contextual challenges, but with entirely different outcomes, what accounts for the difference? We would contend the general difference is one of mindset—and specifically, whether a school has a *scarcity* or an *abundance* mindset.

Only schools that ask good questions can adapt to a rapidly changing world, identify new opportunities, and—in the case of Christian education—live out their missions into the future.

Schools and educators that operate from a scarcity mindset believe that the challenges they face serve to limit who they are and what they do. They perceive the future as uncertain, with the gravity of students' lives weighing in the balance. As such, they tend to ask more closed questions—meaning, the questions they ask do not invite outlying or creative solutions, but keep them stuck within their perceived constraints. Examples of these questions at the teacher level are, How can I be successful at teaching if my students are on so many different levels academically? If the administration can't provide the materials and resources I need for my classroom, how can my students learn? Scarcity-minded questions at the school level might include, How do we enroll more students to make our budget? How can we improve instruction when we can't pay our teachers well enough?

---

3. Angela Duckworth, *Grit: The Power and Passion of Perseverance* (New York, NY: Scribner/Simon & Schuster, 2016).

An abundance mindset looks at the same restraints and challenges, but asks questions that reframe them as opportunities for greater impact. For example, teachers might ask, How can I leverage students' different learning styles and levels and create diverse working groups to tackle projects? What if we reached out to non-profits in the community and partnered together to expand students' learning opportunities through service-learning? From an abundance mindset, leaders might ask, What new opportunities would allow us to expand our reach as a school? What new partnerships—with other schools, churches, ministries, businesses, or community groups—could we forge to do kingdom work together?

As Christian educators, we need to think critically about whether a scarcity mindset or an abundance mindset is more in line with the gospel. We recall the words of Jesus: "The thief comes only to steal and kill and destroy. I came that they may have life and have it abundantly" (John 10:10). There are two insights here that are helpful. The first insight can be found in the second half of the verse, namely that God has made a way for us to live in abundance. He promises that He will "supply every need of yours according to His riches in glory in Christ Jesus" (4:19). In addition to many other similar Scriptures (2 Peter 1:3, Romans 8:32, 1 Timothy 6:17b), the entire arc of Scripture points to a Creator without limits who is rich in love, and who not only sustains but also actively comes to the rescue of His creation. As educators, our default mindset ought to be one of abundance.

An abundance mindset begins with the same restraints and challenges, but reframes them as opportunities for greater impact.

So how is it possible that we could end up with a scarcity mindset? This requires the second insight, which is found in the beginning of the verse. According to John 10:10, the thief is the one who comes to steal, kill, and destroy. To the degree we have a scarcity mindset, it is because we have permitted our mindset of abundance to be stolen away. Often this doesn't happen all at once, but it can be chipped away slowly, over time. Think of the administrator and board that become discouraged from multiple years of declining enrollment, or teachers who feel drained with growing numbers of children each year with challenging emotional and learning needs.

The challenges we face in Christian education are real, and in many cases are difficult and painful. Jesus promised that in this world we would have trouble, but He commanded us to take heart, because He has overcome the world (John 16:33). So what does "taking heart" look like for the Christian educator and Christian school? How do we move forward in an abundance versus a scarcity mindset?

Moving to Abundance

As we mentioned earlier, an abundance mindset begins with the same restraints and challenges, but reframes them as opportunities for greater impact. An opportunity-minded approach leads to openness to new ways of thinking, doing, and being.

This is not just a matter of opinion. Research conducted on award-winning work, done by over 1.7 million corporate employees,[4] suggests that excellence is often inspired by constraints—meaning that employees looked at their constraints (such as rules, policies, and procedures), and rather than giving up, viewed them as a springboard to creative problem-solving.

Further, we can consider how we have all benefited in recent years from the onset of the sharing economy. Consider the value propositions that organizations such as Uber and Airbnb have had on their respective industries. Out of constraints in the transportation and travel industries, creativity gave birth to these innovative, game-changing companies. We need to ask the open-ended question of our own field: In what ways can Christian education's constraints lead to innovation?

To begin to answer this question, the remainder of this chapter will present two case stories. The first provides an illustration of how the faculty at Little Rock Christian Academy intentionally engage

---

4. David Sturt, "Creativity: How Constraints Drive Genius," *Forbes*, (July 12, 2013), accessed May 20, 2019, https://www.forbes.com/sites/groupthink/2013/07/12/creativity-how-constraints-drive-genius/#6e514f8f3d89.

in risk-taking when it comes to teaching and learning. The second shares the story of Open Sky Education, which began in 2002 with 47 students in a single Christian school and has now grown to nearly 11,000 students in private Christian schools, public charter schools, and a wraparound character education project.

Taking Risks Intentionally: Little Rock Christian Academy

An illustration of a school making pedagogical decisions to move from scarcity to abundance is found in Central Arkansas at Little Rock Christian Academy. Nestled in West Little Rock and home to 1,400 students in grades Pk-3-12, Little Rock Christian Academy faculty members embrace an annual Professional Learning Plan (PLP) created by the school's educational team. A significant part of the PLP is based on Jon Eckert's *The Novice Advantage*.[5] Eckert's reflection on practice cycle, or the "4 R's"— reflect, risk, and revise or reject—involves teachers reflecting on their instruction, asking important questions about effectiveness, student engagement, and student inquiry, and building connections on previous concepts. This cycle helps teachers consider the ways in which instructional risk-taking can improve pedagogy and student outcomes.

Teachers at Little Rock Christian Academy annually select an instructional risk that they will focus on throughout the year. For the 2018-2019 year, teachers focused on *developing and assessing a student-centered target risk*. Teachers were to consider instructional practices under the pedagogical umbrella of student-centered learning, including: Harkness discussions; project-based learning; problem-based learning; mastery-based learning assessments; and other collaborative learning activities in which the student is driving much of the learning.

Several faculty members on campus chose to focus specifically on Harkness discussions as target risks for the 2018-2019 PLP. The Harkness method involves the intersection of student-centered and discussion-based learning. Students and their teacher often sit at

---

5. Jon Eckert, *The Novice Advantage: Fearless Practice for Every Teacher* (Thousand Oaks, CA: Corwin, 2016).

a large oval table and engage in academic discourse on a selected text, piece of literature, poem, piece of artwork, or any relevant artifact. The discussions are driven mainly by essential questions and student-generated ideas—creating an atmosphere of authentic learning and genuine curiosity. By the end of the the first semester, teachers provided evidence and artifacts to support their targeted risk and responded to the following prompts: 1) describe how it went; 2) describe the evidence or data you gained; and 3) what will you do differently going forward based on the data? Based on this analysis, many teachers determined that the Harness discussions were a risk worth taking.

The two-fold PLP at Little Rock Christian Academy has been reinforced through on-site professional development led by teachers, which has allowed for quick transfer of knowledge and skill, teacher empowerment, and relationship building all within the context of open-sourcing shared knowledge. Taken together, stronger bonds have grown across campus due to quality time observing and conversing about teaching and learning. Through the process as a whole, teachers are encouraged to take risks—to get outside of their comfort zones and try something new that has the promise of improving student learning. Crucial to this is an atmosphere where risk is corporately encouraged, collaborative support is provided, and fear of failure is mitigated (as in Eckert's model, teachers are able to revise or reject the pedagogy following their experimentation). And intentional risk-taking has created a culture where instructional challenges and limitations are viewed as hurdles to be jumped together, rather than insurmountable walls facing individual teachers.

Intentional risk-taking has created a culture where instructional challenges and limitations are viewed as hurdles to be jumped together, rather than insurmountable walls facing individual teachers.

Another form of partnership that has transformed scarcity into abundance is private-public partnerships in the field of education—specifically, the partnership of privately run schools with public funding. Open Sky Education is one example of an organization that has creatively provided a full and lasting education for children in a model that is affordable and accessible for all, regardless of their income or where they live.

The story of Open Sky Education is the story of God working through His people, leading them to overcome constraints and innovate to meet needs. Open Sky's first school—HOPE Christian School—opened in 2002 with 47 students in Milwaukee, Wisconsin, a city that has been an epicenter for educational innovation since it pioneered one of the nation's first parental voucher programs. When the first HOPE school was born, its founders were striving to grab hold of this new public policy lever—educational vouchers—and use it to address two key challenges in the city of Milwaukee: first, there were significant gaps in academic achievement between economically advantaged and economically disadvantaged students; and second, faith-based schools were closing or consolidating, offering fewer affordable options for Christian education and Christian character role models.

HOPE's founders believed that a full and lasting education was built on three pillars: excellent academics; character formation; and faith formation, if families chose it. They also were determined that this full and lasting education should be accessible and affordable for all, regardless of geography or socioeconomic status. The culture of HOPE is indeed one of abundance: all children can succeed academically and develop strong Christian character, thereby preparing them to live flourishing lives and serve greater purpose.

The idea of limitless potential drove HOPE's founders to find ways to serve more children. When HOPE was launched, voucher programs still were not prevalent in many communities across the

---

6. This case can be found on the Open Sky website and is used with permission; accessed May 23, 2019, https://openskyeducation.org/an-amazing-journey.

country, yet the needs were great. Delivering the three pillars to more children became the mission; growth with quality and sustainability became the vision.

Scanning the educational landscape, these innovative leaders continued to leverage public policy and innovative thinking, which ultimately led to the development of public charter schools (EAGLE College Preparatory Schools) in communities seeking high-quality charter school providers. EAGLE schools deliver the excellent academics and character formation pillars of Open Sky's mission. For parents also desiring the third pillar—faith formation—Open Sky developed a separate organization to provide Christian wraparound care in the form of before- and after-school care and preschool programming provided by Compass Educational Programs.

Although it was a startup organization with evolving names through the years, Open Sky's mission and innovative spirit have remained constant. Since its inception, Open Sky has grown to serve more than 5,000 children in its private Christian schools as well as public charter schools that have a separate option for Christian wraparound care for families in neighborhoods with limited economic resources. Beyond the students and educators in its own schools, Open Sky serves an additional 6,000 students in partnering public schools and private Christian schools with its Character Formation Project. A total of eight Open Sky campuses with EAGLE and Compass programs are located in Phoenix, Arizona and St. Louis, Missouri. The Character Formation Project is embedded within each campus: civic curriculum for the public charter schools, and Christian curriculum for the Compass programs.

All children can succeed academically and develop strong Christian character, thereby preparing them to live flourishing lives and serve greater purpose.

As the organization grew, it adopted a new name—Open Sky Education—more fitting of the entrepreneurial spirit that is in the hearts of its serving leaders, and the limitless potential of providing a full and lasting education for children in models that are accessible and affordable for all. It is a name causing our eyes to look to the heavens, the source from which abundant blessings and opportunities flow to serve His children. And with the shifts they see in public policy (allowing billions of dollars in public funding to be used by families to access privately-run educational options) and technology, which knows no geographic nor financial constraints, the team at Open Sky Education believes we may be living at one of the most opportune times in the history of the world to be in the field of Christian education.

Beyond the Horizon

In 1961, what lay beyond the horizon for the United States was, quite literally, the moon. President Kennedy and his cabinet could have tried to improve the American space program with a broad generic claim, yet it was most effective for President Kennedy to state the following specific, measurable goal: "This nation should commit itself to achieving the goal, before this decade is out, of landing a man on the moon and returning him safely to earth."[7]

That goal was achieved with Neil Armstrong's famous first step roughly eight years later, on July 20, 1969. President Kennedy's "moon shot" worked. Such a bold claim by the president at that point in the nation's history became a powerful motivation to move vigorously forward in overcoming what, up until that point, seemed to be an insurmountable challenge and limitation.

Christian schools today face challenges and opportunities in a rapidly changing world, which makes it all the more important for each organization to think critically about the areas in which having less can lead to having more. In other words, current limitations should not be a disadvantage to Christian schools, if leaders and educators are willing to consider them as opportunities. If we change our mindset in this way, we can position ourselves for the abundance that God has provided and will continue to provide. Moving from

---

7. "May 25, 1961: JFK's Moonshot Speech to Congress" *Space.com*, accessed May 25, 2019, https://www.space.com/11772-president-kennedy-historic-speech-moon-space.html.

scarcity to abundance requires that we look beyond the horizon, define our "moon shot," and then take it—in faith.

Questions for Discussion

1. What inspiration for your own classroom and school can you take from the questioning techniques used by Jesus—open-ended, frequently provocative, and rarely answered by Him?

2. What does an abundance mindset mean to you? Is it just all the "good" things? What does abundance mean in the face of challenges, disappointment, or despair? What holds you back from living fully from an abundance mindset?

3. What examples of behaviors in your school might reflect a scarcity mindset? Conversely, what examples of behaviors in your school might reflect an abundance mindset?

4. What insights or inspiration did you take away from the stories of Little Rock Christian Academy and Open Sky Education in this chapter?

5. What does the "moon shot" look like when it comes to your classroom or your school? In other words, what opportunities are you facing that will require an abundance mindset— believing in God's goodness and provision—if you are to grab hold of them?

6. How might risk-taking in Christian schools reflect a Christian understanding of the world? What practical steps could you take to enable yourself and your colleagues to take risks together?

From Isolated to Networked

Andy Wolfe

In 1811, Joshua Watson, a church leader in London, gathered together a group of like-minded individuals with a vision for their churches creating free educational institutions to serve the children of their parishes. At this point in time, there was no access to education for families who could not pay for it. Thus the Church of England globally pioneered the provision of learning experiences for families of every socioeconomic background, opening schools which grew quickly in size and popularity, spreading across England through the Church of England's parish system.

It was a culture-changing moment of social justice that would change the nation's approach to education and go on to influence educational provision on a global scale. Over 200 years later, the Church of England oversees just under 5000 schools, educating over one million children representing approximately 20% of the English education system—quite a remarkable engagement of church and state and a pervasive opportunity for a Christian vision for education to impact the lives of young people.

Readers outside of the English context may imagine that it would be fairly easy to connect Church of England schools one with another for the purpose of sharing common curricula, pedagogical practice, and overall vision for children's flourishing. In fact, the opposite is true. Because the Church of England operates in a way in which there are 41 dioceses across the country, and every diocese has its own bishop and education team, there is no centralized command and control structure. Put simply, Church of England schools are not franchises. (We like to say we've looked around the church's national education office for a lever to pull to get everybody to do something, and it just doesn't exist, because that's not how the Church of England functions.)

The question becomes, then, how to generate ideas and ways of working together that are so contagious and attractive that people throughout our schools say, "Yes, that's exactly who we are, and what we want to do!" This has become vitally important in the current season of increasing pressure and accountability for schools, where the need to define the identity, purpose, and ethos of a school (or group/network of schools) continues to increase.

As we have moved toward greater community engagement by way of shared vision and practices, we are finding that educators who don't necessarily hold our same faith position are attracted to what we're doing—that the Christian narrative offers a genuinely attractive vision for education.

What follows is the four-year story of how Church of England schools first articulated a shared vision of education and then developed support for school leadership and peer networks in order to actualize that shared vision. While Church of England schools have always been on the journey toward greater engagement as a community, we have been humbled by the opportunity to travel together with our schools and colleagues in this most recent chapter of the story. It is our hope that the insights shared here can inspire educators in their own journeys as they seek to overcome isolation and build networks of practice.

A Shared Vision

Our journey started with the need to more clearly define the "why" of Church of England education, rather than simply articulating the "what" of schools' activity. Even though the Church had been involved in education for many years, what had never been done was to articulate and write down the Church's unique vision for education, including why education is important to the Church. This meant Church of England schools lacked a statement around which educators could convene.

To this end, and following significant consultation with educational stakeholders and Church leaders, the Church of England Vision for Education, *Deeply Christian, Serving the Common Good*,[1] was published in Autumn 2016. The Vision document seeks to define the "why" of education, and offers an attractive, aspirational, and inclusive vision for education. It is an expansive vision for education for all schools, not just those run by the Church of England.

The Vision for Education takes John 10:10 as a central text— "Life in all its fullness"—and asks if Jesus came to bring life in all of its fullness, what kind of education would be necessary in order to equip children and young people to be able to embrace and discover that life? In answering that question, the Vision identifies four dimensions essential to an educational ecology that is sufficient for such fullness:

- **Educating for Wisdom, Knowledge and Skills**—Fostering discipline, confidence and delight in seeking wisdom and knowledge (including a healthy and life-giving tension between knowledge-rich and biblical wisdom curriculum approaches), and fully developing talents in all areas of life.
- **Educating for Hope and Aspiration**—Seeking healing, repair and renewal, coping wisely with things and people going wrong, opening horizons and guiding people into ways of fulfilling them.
- **Educating for Community and Living Well Together**— Ensuring a core focus on relationships, participation in communities, and the qualities of character that enable people to flourish together.

---

1. Church of England, "Vision for Education," accessed May 21, 2019, https://www.churchofengland.org/more/education-and-schools/vision-education.

- **Educating for Dignity and Respect**—Ensuring the basic principle of respect for the value and preciousness of each person, treating each person as a unique individual of inherent worth.

The document outlines these in layers of multiple depths, beginning with an inclusive overview of the four concepts, followed by a rich Christian theological underpinning of the terms and their practical application in education, drawing on a wide range of biblical thinking. Altogether, the Vision pushes us to move beyond knowledge for knowledge's sake, to equipping students with the wisdom of character to be able to live out that knowledge in such a way that makes a deeply Christian impact on society.

A competition-based approach isn't in line with the economy of God's kingdom. More commensurate with that kingdom is an approach focused on community-building.

Nearly three years after its release, the Vision has been warmly welcomed and embraced by school leaders across England, illustrating the importance of defining the core purpose or "why" of education. This is largely because it has been viewed not as a rigid set of guidelines with which to straitjacket schools, but rather a critical lens through which educators can view their own local practice. Leaders view it as inherently attractive and immediately useful in their own work in faculty development and school improvement. As we travel around the country and visit individual dioceses, we are finding, whether in Manchester, Cornwall, or Birmingham, leaders are finding the Vision's language to be hospitable and inclusive.

Moreover, we are finding that there is something powerful that happens when Church of England schools—and increasingly schools that aren't church schools—can identify with the same visioning nationally. Specifically, a shared language helps educators to move beyond our personal "why's," to a rationale that is bigger than individuals and therefore naturally connects us with others. It also inspires us to excellence and further action (for example, schools are now able to use the Vision as a framework for the U.K. inspection process[2]).

As exciting as the unifying work we have seen within Church of England schools is, we have also experienced newfound and expanded opportunities for influencing the educational discourse both nationally and internationally. As we have moved toward greater community engagement by way of shared vision and practices, we are finding that educators who don't necessarily hold our same faith position are attracted to what we're doing—that the Christian narrative offers a genuinely attractive vision for education.

Ethos-Enhanced Leadership

In a similar fashion, as we have been invited outside of the U.K. to share this story, we have found several applications of our experience in the international context. Some schools internationally do not have a clear articulation of their organizational purpose, while others have a statement of their purpose either long-standing from the school's inception, or re-visited according to current leadership opinions. In many Christian schools, these words may have an implicit or explicit biblical underpinning, or link to particular local church traditions.

Regardless of the words that are used to describe a school's statement of purpose—perhaps a mission, vision, or values statement—we are most interested in a school's "ethos," or a school's leadership-driven DNA that determines their identity, priorities, and decision-making. However this character is defined, it is imperative the school's ethos is shared and owned by the whole community. Anything that is worth building cannot be built alone.

Secondly, a direct and influential connection should be established between the ethos and the pursuit of outcomes sought by the school. If the ethos does not impact the decision-making of leaders, it is arguably not the ethos at all but rather a set of words on a wall, or bullet points in a policy document. Our organizational ethos is demonstrated in our decision-making, evidenced in our schedules

---

2. Similar to accreditation processes in other countries.

and budgets, and frequently revealed most powerfully in our most challenging circumstances. When leadership decisions are driven by a clear ethos, an organization's pursuit of improved outcomes is improved and enhanced—including for example academic performance in external assessment, the design of a curriculum, the development of students' character, or the stewardship of resources and budgeting decisions.

Accompanying the Church of England Vision for Education, we have published a large suite of leadership development resources in this area, for leaders at different levels, including local school leaders, system leaders, and those engaged in educational governance. The documents are based on a series of provocative questions, using a Socratic model, and are designed to underpin leadership development within individual institutions, and across local and national network groups. While they use the four pillars of the Church of England Vision for Education as their basis, the vast majority of questions are easily transferred into other contexts. The questioning approach is very open-ended, enabling clear focus on a particular school leadership issue while allowing creative space for leaders to interact and co-construct their own collaborative work.

A parallel resource takes a more coaching-based starting point for consideration of school leadership issues, drawing together leaders' thinking in three interacting domains of leadership, pedagogy, and theology. This allows leaders to reflect together in peer groups as leaders, teachers, and theologians; the interdisciplinary approach is very effective at drawing together leaders from different backgrounds (including the engagement of church leaders in educational thinking from a theological starting point, and indeed early career teachers who are not yet in leadership roles). This again supports leaders in the sharing and co-ownership of vision.

Peer Support Networks

As we think about the MindShift approach in North America, an area of our work that seems to offer significant potential is that of school-to-school support and peer networking. Our Peer Support Network was established and piloted in 2016-17, growing quickly from 66 schools in the first year, to 150 schools in year two, with now in 2018-19, over 700 schools involved in the network across England. This rapid growth is encouraging and evidences a growing desire for school leaders to support, encourage, and challenge one another's development in focused peer groups.

While schools and educators in different countries or regions may be connected by proximity or associational affiliation, to operate deliberately within a networked community of practice is an entirely different ballgame—because to do so means acknowledging that the solution to our problem is probably held by somebody around the table. This is fundamentally different from trying to compete with the people around the table, which is often the more prevalent dynamic in education discourse; the marketization of education creates a dynamic where schools are supposed to perform and outdo each other, in a zero-sum game.

The problem of course is that a competition-based approach isn't in line with the economy of God's kingdom. More commensurate with that kingdom is an approach focused on community-building. Along these lines, we have found that good leaders are naturally looking for best practices, but they are also seeking to contribute.

Networking facilitates sustained collaboration and generates a sense of a genuine community of practice.

A genuine network enables educators to ask and then answer the question, What can I contribute to this, as well as what can I get out of it? Fundamentally, this reciprocity is the difference between facilitating a network and running a program.

There are a number of key pieces of learning now emerging around the effectiveness of Peer Support Networks; we chose to highlight four.

1. **Sharing and Ownership of Focus.** Although broadly speaking most schools recognize the need and attraction of collaboration, networking needs a clear focus for it to be effective and to become embedded in the leadership journey within and between schools. The Foundation's networks have

established foci in two complementary ways: school category/context (for example, where schools from similar socio-economic or geographical contexts come together to work specifically on leadership issues pertaining to their shared context); and common development focus (where schools gather around a shared leadership development priority, such as curriculum design, character education, faith development, budget/resources.) Without the coalescence around one or both of these elements, however well-intentioned the networking is, it can be susceptible to fading out quickly. The early establishment of trust, vulnerability, and sharing is crucial, alongside the pragmatic need for "quick wins" whereby school leaders are able to identify (and share with others) early on, the actual benefits they have received from being part of the network.

2. Expert Facilitation with High-Quality Resources. Effective networks are not linear programs to be delivered but responsive learning journeys realized in mutually beneficial relationships. While it is important to have a structure and goal, the skill of facilitation is quite different to that of delivering a course or module. The Peer Support Network is facilitated regionally by experienced and credible school leaders who combine the ability to draw on their own leadership development journey with the facilitation of high-quality learning experiences using the very best national resources. This network provides a powerful value-added proposition to leaders, who recognize that they are receiving insight and input at a national level, while co-constructing their shared leadership development narrative locally.

3. Clear Logistics and School-Based Delivery. Although there is a justification for a national gathering or conference, the vast majority of successful network groups are locally delivered and reliant on easy geographical and transportation connections. A series of events are all based in schools (rather than a hotel or training suite) in order to remain fully embedded in the life of the school, and they always involve the opportunity for a leadership-focus tour, alongside discussion and networking activity. Between events, leaders engage in tasks, such as development activities, to be brought back to the following session. In some cases, this has been helpfully supported by video conferencing experiences.

4. Longer-Term Commitment and Developing a Movement. While the demand for rapid leadership development and school improvement is a clear part of our educational discourse, the greatest impact of the Peer Support Network has been seen through requiring a commitment beyond one academic year. This establishes a more realistic and encouraging relational engagement between leaders and also empowers leaders to focus on longer-term priorities. And as the networks grow over time, relational capital is exchanged, allowing relationships to grow through a variety of seasons. Leaders willing to invest for the longer term are far more likely to ask the broader questions on entry, including fundamentally considering not simply what can I gain, but also what can I give?

In our experience, when we focus on the right things (meaning things that people are already working on), and provide them with a new language and new energy to enhance what they're doing (rather than just making a different version of what they're doing), we are able to create an attractive environment in which leaders are eager to network. And in this context, networking facilitates sustained collaboration and generates a sense of a genuine community of practice.

Flourishing Communities

Finally we turn to revisit the opening central text of the Vision for Education, Jesus' promise of "life in all its fullness" in John 10:10. There are many proxy measures of success for education—attendance, examination results, college entry, athletic accomplishments, artistic achievement, financial sustainability—but even in combination these may not tell the full picture of the kind of education we seek. "Life in all its fullness" leads us towards a notion of "flourishing" that is a helpfully inclusive concept for a broader and deeper view of what education is all about.

A Christian understanding of flourishing is firmly grounded in the teaching of Jesus and expansively illustrated through a wide range of parables and examples. We may consider, for example, the Parable of the Sower, Abiding in the Vine, and the Mustard Seed. Indeed the metaphor of trees planted by living waters and their subsequent bearing of fruit extends right back to the Old Testament prophets (Jeremiah 17) and the Psalms (Psalm 1 and others).

While our goal may well be flourishing children, for this to be achieved, we must also focus on leadership development and flourishing teachers and leaders. There may be few flourishing children where there are few flourishing adults. For Church of England schools, our main efforts to promote flourishing have been through crafting an attractive shared vision, strengthening ethos-enhanced leadership, and facilitating authentic and collaborative peer support networks. While your school and geographic setting may be very different from ours, moving from isolation to networked communities will no doubt be key for flourishing in your context.

Questions for Discussion

1. How do you articulate your personal vision for education, and what variance might there be in your school among teachers, leaders, and staff?

2. What do you understand by "life in all its fullness," and how might young people experience this in your school?

3. To what extent does your school's ethos actively enhance its pursuit of outcomes? How would anyone know if they visited your classrooms, board meetings, or read your schedule or budgets?

4. Who is your tribe/network? With whom do you find resonance, and how could you build networks locally, regionally, or nationally?

5. What excites you about networking, and what might you

consider committing to as a result? What are the costs, and what are the opportunities? What are the challenges of networking in relation to competition between institutions?

6. Do you approach networking thinking what can I receive, or what can I give?

7. What kind of networking practices might be identified as deeply Christian?

From White to Mosaic

By Michael Chen, Jenny Brady, and Joel Gaines

Christ-centered education is at a crossroads. One path seems straightforward and familiar—leading to a perceived sense of cultural and religious safety. The other path seems to lead to the unknown—appearing muddy and winding through interactions with people and perspectives seemingly different from ourselves. As educators, the path we choose is reflected in all that we do: from our admissions policies, which impact demographics of the student body and signal which kinds of families belong at our school; to faculty hiring practices that ultimately shape the learning environment; to curricular decisions that determine what and how our students learn.

We contend that traveling down the second path is fundamental to a Christ-centered way of knowing and believing, essential to staying on mission, and necessary to be culturally relevant in the 21st century. This messy and risky endeavor of re-imagining Christ-centered education in an increasingly interconnected world aims to challenge our assumptions about the interplay between diversity and the aim of education. While in this chapter we focus specifically on the knowledge base we need to engage racial and cultural diversity in our schools, we believe the principles we uncover encourage us as educators in the broader conversation about what it means for us to be created in the Imago Dei—with varying nationalities, languages, abilities, and lived experiences—as well as who are our neighbors (Luke 10:29) and what it means to love them (Mark 12:31).

Building Our Own Houses

First, we invite you to imagine this scenario with us. Six-year old Jack and five-year old Toni are playing with Lego bricks together. They each build a house; Toni's house is built with colorful bricks and Jack's house with white bricks. With great satisfaction, they relish in their own creativity and accomplishment and look to their teacher for their next challenge. The teacher then asks them to use the Lego bricks that they have and build one house together. They respond to the challenge enthusiastically, look to each other, and wonder how to begin.

The question is: do they tear down both houses, re-imagine a new house together, and then use all the bricks, both colorful and white, to build this new house? Does Toni tear down her colorful house and put her colorful bricks on Jack's white house?

This scenario is reflective of complex questions about diversity, pluralism, and racial relations in our U.S. society in its historical context. For example, who is in charge of deciding what bricks to keep and what to get rid of? Whose vision of the new house will serve as the blueprint? Who has the power to decide on the rules of the game that Jack and Toni play? These are the key diversity questions that we need to ask, but are *not* asking at the moment in most of our Christian schools.

Rather, we frequently hear well-intentioned colleagues in Christian education state that it is time to "move beyond the race conversation" and that their schools are lovingly serving and celebrating all God's children, regardless of background. Yet, when we try to bring diverse students into Christian schools without thoughtful plans for engagement and integration, many students of color ultimately feel the pressure to break up their colorful houses and place their blocks on the white Lego house. In other words, they quickly realize that they must play by someone else's rules and assimilate to a dominant white culture.

While Christian schools may genuinely aim to serve all

students, too often many students from diverse backgrounds feel voiceless and are not given the opportunity to imagine and shape their school communities. The Lego illustration shows that striving for diversity is not enough. In this chapter we discuss how we must, and how we can, do more.

David Brooks of the New York Times once wrote of many kinds of societal divides (such as rich/poor, urban/rural, red/blue). In his reflections, he states that "the racial divide doesn't feel like the other divides. There is a dimension of depth to it that the other divides don't have. It is more central to the American experience."[1] We agree with this observation—our nation's history demands us to confront and engage with issues of racial justice and diversity. And, as Christ-followers and educators, we take this a step further: seeking racial and cultural diversity in our human experience is essential to the discipleship life that God calls us to live, as it provides us with lessons on learning and knowing in the context of education.

While Christian schools may genuinely aim to serve all students, too often many students from diverse backgrounds feel voiceless and are not given the opportunity to imagine and shape their school communities.

At the start, we recognize that when talking about racial and cultural diversity, people come to the conversation with varying levels of comfort and buy-in. Some may come to the conversation having seen first-hand the power of bringing diverse human perspectives and experiences together, and therefore may view diversity as fundamental to building transformative communities. Yet others may view diversity as a nice ideal for which to strive, but not at the expense of maintaining a clear set of norms and cultural stability. Engaging in the process of unpacking and embracing racial and cultural diversity can simultaneously bring out the best and the most vulnerable parts in us, as we work through

---

1. David Brooks, "The Case for Reparations," *New York Times*, March 7, 2019, accessed May 21, 2019, https://www.nytimes.com/2019/03/07/opinion/case-for-reparations.html.

the many historical implications that inform how we all live and interact today. Yet, we hope you will hear our stories and ideas with open minds and hearts, to see what God might be stirring in you as you consider the value of diversity in Christ-centered education and nurturing future generations of Christ followers.

Building on the Foundation

Educators spend most of their time working with knowledge. We teach students to know subjects, know themselves, know each other, and know the world around them. But rarely do we ask the question of what it means to *know* something or, more specifically, some *one*. A deeper understanding is needed as a foundation for doing the work we discuss in this chapter. Lesslie Newbigin, a British theologian and missionary, offered this insight:

> But there is another kind of knowing…It is the kind of knowing that we seek in our relations with other people. In this kind of knowing we are not in full control. We may ask questions, but we must also answer the questions put by the other. We can only come to know others in the measure of which they are willing to share. The resulting knowledge is not simply our own achievement; it is also the gift of others.[2]

This type of "knowing" is crucial for our students—and for ourselves as educators—to develop. Our turbulent world is full of broken relationships. We are often surrounded by only the voices with which we already agree, making it easy to just ignore or write off people with different perspectives. Yet, Christ calls us to something different—to love our neighbors as ourselves. To be effective, Christ-centered teachers and leaders, we must equip our students to lovingly engage with people who come from communities, life experiences, and perspectives different from their own—without presumption or expectation, but rather with the desire to truly know them.

---

2. Lesslie Newbigin, *Proper Confidence: Faith, Doubt, and Certainty in Christian Discipleship* (Grand Rapids: Wm. B. Eerdmans Publishing, 1995), 10.

Similarly, our knowledge and understanding of God, which is built on our ongoing relationship with Him, gives shape for how we interpret and understand the world around us. We wonder if this is part of what Paul says in Colossians, that "[Christ] is before all things and in him all things hold together" (Colossians 1:17). When we get to know Christ more though a lifetime of discipleship, things in life would make more sense to us because "in him all [meaning] holds together."

Curiously, the story of us knowing God begins with the premise that we, as human beings, are incapable of knowing the true God. Christian faith asserts that divine understanding is not something we strive for or are able to achieve on our own; this is the biggest existential and epistemological divide—God and human beings. Only God can bridge this divide. And he did. Christ did so by relinquishing his privileges and "made himself nothing, taking on the very nature of a servant, being made in human likeness" (Philippians 2:7). God's way of loving us is through his committed act of sacrifice, through the lowering of himself to humanity, and by bridging the fundamentally unbridgeable divide.

To be effective, Christ-centered teachers and leaders, we must equip our students to lovingly engage with people who come from communities, life experiences, and perspectives different from their own—without presumption or expectation, but rather with the desire to truly know them.

So, what are the implications of God bridging the impossible divide? As Paul reminds us in 2 Corinthians, because of his reconciliation work and the divine diversity of God's family, "he gave us the ministry of reconciliation" with others in this life (2 Corinthians 5:18). He calls us to bridge the divide between others and us, even when it might seem difficult. The way that God came to know us, knowing even "the hairs in our heads" (Matthew 10:30) serves to give us the shape of knowing, or pattern of knowing others, whether it is people or subjects or the world around us, so that we know how to properly, thoughtfully, and redemptively relate to others who are different from us.

Furthermore, how this is important to Christ-centered education is that we must provide opportunities for our students to *learn from* those who are different from them and *learn with* those who are different from them. We must communicate that bridging the divide between people for the love of knowing is fundamental to our faith journey. Our students will lose out on this important dimension of their discipleship life if they don't engage thoughtfully, intentionally, and redemptively with other students of different racial, cultural, and linguistic backgrounds. Moreover, diversity in school allows many students of privileged backgrounds to learn how to relinquish their privilege, attentively listen to others' stories, and attentively and lovingly develop genuine relationships with others.

We must provide opportunities for our students to learn from those who are different from them and learn with those who are different from them.

This is our case for racial and ethnic diversity in our schools. However, a case requires evidence, or authentic stories, to illustrate principles in action. We are humbled and privileged to work or have worked at three Christian schools, whose stories of transformation are illustrative of what is needed to journey toward truly mosaic communities. Before we share them, however, we want to emphasize that "unless the Lord builds the house, those who build it labor in vain" (Psalm 127:1). In each case, these schools' stories center on God's Spirit and His activity in the life of educators, families, and the school community at large. These schools—Prestonwood Christian Academy, The City School, and Boston Trinity Academy—are God's building projects, not ours. As we invite you into these stories, we're reminded that it is God who graciously invited each of us into His story of building diversity, shalom, and justice at each of these schools, respectively.

Building Toward Diversity: Prestonwood Christian Academy

Back in 2001, Prestonwood Christian Academy (PCA), located in the suburbs of Dallas, Texas, was in its fifth year as a school and about to graduate its first class, comprised of only eight students. Jenny remembers sitting in the teacher's lounge one morning and spotting the school's new marketing magazine on the table, with a diverse array of students of all ages and racial and cultural backgrounds. Because the photo was not truly representative of school's current demographics, it stirred in Jenny a thought—what if they were able to develop a school that reflected God's design for Heaven in which every tribe and nation are represented, as we trained students in their knowledge and love of Christ and equip them to make disciples for him? Not only was this a part of God's call for all believers, but also an intentional focus on diversity could be a key component of the school's mission to attract and educate students from a variety of backgrounds.

Along with school leadership, Jenny began to prayerfully imagine what a diversity program would entail. Together with a few board members, they searched for best practices of developing diversity programs for Christian schools in the Dallas area—but soon learned that neither in Dallas nor in all of Texas was there a Christian primary, secondary, or university-level school with a diversity program. Because of that, they began contacting other non-religious independent schools in the area to learn from the ones with diversity programs.

During this year the leadership also joined with teachers, parents, and board members to wrestle prayerfully with their understanding of diversity in a Christ-centered way. Together, they recognized that they weren't dealing with mere demographic categories but rather with students created in God's image. Wanting to provide a safe and comfortable learning environment for all students in a wide range of diversity categories, they established the definition of diversity through the acronym "GRACE"—which stands for **G**ender (male and female), **R**ace, **A**ge, **A**bility (academic and physical ability), **C**ulture, and **E**conomic status.

As time went on, PCA's sensitivity toward building an equitable and diverse school went beyond numbers. For example, the leaders and faculty quickly realized that they were teaching from one cultural narrative, planning events and programs with assumptions and understanding of only one group's experiences and desires, and creating systems that met the needs of just one group of people. PCA made the difficult but intentional journey from a perspective that wasn't inclusive of everyone at the school—nor of those they desired to be at the school—to being proactive about reflecting diversity in the curriculum, athletic and fine arts programs, development and business departments, school events, and school policies and procedures.

PCA changed dramatically over the following years. Not only has PCA grown into a system of five schools and increased in overall enrollment, but also the percentage of racial minority students has grown from 7% in 2008 to 28% in 2019. As it has become an increasingly diverse school, it reflects the Revelation vision of God's kingdom. But more important than numbers, as PCA works toward equity, inclusion, understanding, and appreciation, it better and more authentically reflects the promise of John 13:35, "By this all people will know that you are my disciples, if you have love for one another."

Since becoming intentional about diversity, PCA's admissions policies haven't changed—but some procedures have. PCA's curriculum standards haven't changed—but some of the stories teachers share in their classes have. PCA's mission statement and portrait of a graduate hasn't changed—but how those are actualized sometimes has. Change wasn't always easy, and the initial years were filled with initial growing pains, impatience, and frustration. However, a board member's encouragement from Psalm 65:9, that "God has to prepare the field for the blessings he will bring," has been foundational for developing a perspective of patience. While some at the school were passionate about diversity, it was important to take the time to bring others along and recognize that not everyone will understand why or what is being done, and that is part of the process of educating others. Above all, it encouraged confidence in God's desire to move hearts of people in the school's direction to diversity.

Building Toward Shalom: The City School

Along with cheesesteaks, the Rocky steps, and the Liberty Bell, Philadelphia is known for birthing Insomnia Cookies, a bakery that will deliver hot, freshly-baked cookies 24 hours a day. If you walk past Insomnia Cookies, or perhaps even your favorite bakery, you can usually catch a whiff of something delicious that draws you in—often no other advertisement is necessary. Fundamentally, this is what Christian schools could be: as we engage in conversations around diversity rooted in the beauty of the image of God (Imago Dei), the aroma of Christ (Psalm 34:8) would permeate the surrounding communities and draw people in.

Located in Philadelphia, The City School has an ambitious mission to serve the diverse student population of the city and a commitment to provide quality Christian urban education. A joint merger of three urban schools, The City School carries with it these three schools' legacies to serve students in the city of Philadelphia through excellent and accessible education. This translates into the school's five core commitments: to Jesus, to shalom, to the city, to excellence, and to accessibility.

As we engage in conversations around diversity rooted in the beauty of the image of God (Imago Dei), the aroma of Christ (Psalm 34:8) would permeate the surrounding communities and draw people in.

Working toward all of these commitments is highly aspirational and challenging. As the high school principal at the school's brand new secondary campus, Joel has found it uniquely to be the case in working to bring *shalom*, God's peace, to students and the city from which they come. The idea of shalom is significant in talking about race, ethnicity, and culture in many Christian school communities because of the cognitive dissonance, discomfort, or pain that accompany such topics. It is no exception at The City School. In the process of working with teachers and staff in developing their ability to bring shalom to the urban school setting, Joel focuses on four

"C's": *courage*; *communication*; *cultural humility*; and *Christ-centered commitment*.

Talking about race and racial diversity points squarely to the conflicts between people in the context of the history of the United States. Therefore, we need *courage* to engage people in talking through the pain of our racial history, and to make connections between that history and the current racial disparities in education, opportunity, income, and more. Courage at The City School has included asking teachers to read challenging books for professional development, like *For White Folks Who Teach in the Hood...and the Rest of Y'all Too*.[3] The school year also starts with anti-racism training led by organizations dedicated to make schools a safe and inclusive place for all students. Understandably, racial conversations in these trainings can become difficult and tense, when teachers are learning to have courage to confront their own assumptions and challenge themselves to be the kind of educators that will serve their diverse student body well. As teachers increase their awareness of their own cultural identities and assumptions in the context of a diverse setting, they are more likely to be God's effective instrument to bring shalom to their students.

Another important way for the school to move beyond simply building diversity is effective *communication* in this diverse setting. The head of school would speak humbly about his cultural identity (white) and honestly about how he contends with the tension of being a white person leading a majority-minority school. Such authentic communication builds trust from all school stakeholders and the surrounding communities. Teachers also have learned attentiveness, active listening, and intentionality when speaking, which allows them to also earn trust from their students who may be different from them culturally.

At The City School, *cultural humility* is defined as a lifelong process of self-reflection and awareness with a respectful attitude toward diverse points of view. Early in the school's journey of moving beyond diversity toward a deeper multicultural understanding,

---

3. Christopher Emdin, *For White Folks Who Teach in the Hood... and the Rest of Y'all Too: Reality Pedagogy and Urban Education* (Boston, MA: Beacon Press, 2016).

teachers often worried about inadvertently offending others by saying the wrong things or using the wrong words. As a result, teachers either became quiet or they could not advance the conversations beyond the superficial. Together, leadership and faculty had to work hard to develop a norm of understanding: that we all have room to grow in how we relate to others, and that we all need to learn from others by earnestly asking questions.

Finally, with courage to seek *shalom* in others, communication grounded in our compassion for others, and cultural humility to grow in our service to others, the school community moves beyond diversity and begins to answer Micah 6:8's calling to "do justice, love mercy, and walk humbly before our God." The City School hasn't arrived yet, but has the *Christ-centered commitment* to press on to cultivate the fragrant aroma of shalom.

Building Toward a Just Community: Boston Trinity Academy

After a successful decade-long endeavor to develop a diverse school in Boston, educators at Boston Trinity Academy sought to go beyond their initial focus on diversity to re-imagine an equitable and justice-oriented school premised on racial reconciliation. Boston Trinity's diverse student body, comprised of a third of the student body identifying as white, another third black, and another third Asian, Latino, and others, came with complex and often conflict-prone relationships between students and between students and their teachers.

Together with a team of graduating 12th grade students in 2012, Michael began designing a reconciliation program aiming to address the class culture of that year's junior class. At that point, most teachers considered this class to be the most racially divided and racially charged class in the school's history to date. In responding to the Apostle Paul's call to ministry of reconciliation in 2 Corinthians, Michael set out to train the 12th grade students to be student trainers on racial reconciliation. In this train-the-trainers cascade approach, the students discussed how to deconstruct toxic norms and reconstruct a healthy culture. They practiced listening to each other openly, bracketing their preconceived ideas of others. And, they facilitated vulnerable openness with one another to allow students to genuinely be known by one another.

Once the seniors were trained, they conducted a one-week intensive training for the junior class, by facilitating a series of community building exercises ranging from fun and superficial to serious and thought-provoking. Students were surprised by their peers' personal stories—and engaged in shattering stereotypes, challenging assumptions, and penetrating the stronghold of ignorance. The iterative dive from listening to others intently, to sharing personal stories with others vulnerably, gave these students the insight into how different they were from each other. And yet, they also realized that they shared so much in common as well—from personal struggles, conflicts in relationships, complicated circumstances in families, joy and sorrows found in friendships, the longing to be loved and the desire to love someone, and many other human experiences. As the training progressed, it was evident that dividing walls between students were crumbling. And by the end, not a single student was without tears. They asked for forgiveness from each other, celebrated their newfound understanding of one another, committed to building a loving and supporting community together, and found inspiration from these experiences to lead the rest of the school by example when they came back as seniors the following year.

It is important for students, faculty, and staff to articulate diverse stories, ask hard questions, and listen intently and without assumption.

At the time, Michael did not know if this transformative experience was simply unique to this class of students or if this transformation could take place again with other groups of students. However, after a similar experience happened again to the next junior class the following year, he realized he had stumbled into an effective practice to build common ground in diversity. Such authentic and intense reconciliatory experiences continue to transform every junior class every year since then. Even after Michael left the school in 2015 to become the head of another school, Boston Trinity Academy built upon these principles of deconstruction and reconstruction by broadening the reconciliation work to impact the entire school community. This time, the head of school led the charge and truly exemplified the best of all the essential elements of cultural humility, authenticity, and vulnerability, as the school journeyed on the road to build a beautiful, collaborative mosaic.

Building Together

As we conclude this chapter, we return to the illustration with which we began. When we look at our two Lego houses that exist at many Christian schools, what do we do? What does it mean to deconstruct both houses to create a collaborative mosaic? We'd like to offer three suggestions for beginning this journey together.

First, we must *acknowledge that the two houses exist, and that they are distinct from one another*. The overwhelming majority of our Christian schools were established with White societal norms and cultural assumptions. When this goes unrecognized or unacknowledged, our students of color will continue to feel the need to assimilate to this culture in order to succeed in this context. And those who benefit from the current house structure feel comfortable and generally do not feel a need to change the house.

Second, we need to *critically analyze each house and learn about each builder*. Paraphrasing the words of Ta-Nehisi Coates, our quest from "White to Mosaic" is not the acceptance of our differences (or, as in much of our American meta-narrative, the white acceptance of others); rather, it is the acceptance of our collective story and its consequences.[4] In this stage, it is important for students, faculty, and staff to articulate diverse stories, ask hard questions, and listen intently and without assumption. Our goal must be to seek the reconciliation of relationships, the restoration of broken systems, and the repentance of historical and contemporary injustices and sins that

---

4. Ta-Nehisi Coates, "The Case for Reparations," *The Atlantic* (June 2014), accessed May 22, 2019, https://www.theatlantic.com/magazine/archive/2014/06/the-case-for-reparations/361631/.

created and perpetuated these divisions in the first place.

Finally, we *mutually deconstruct each house and reconstruct a collaborative, colorful mosaic with mutual trust and understanding.* In the context of a Christ-centered school, diverse perspectives come together to re-imagine a school, being attentive to the tacit concerns of those who tend to be voiceless and powerless. We need to re-negotiate how we play together and how we can design this house together—and empower all to envision a school community where *shalom* and flourishing are possible for everyone.

Philosopher Simone Weil once wrote, "Love sees what is invisible."[5] Seeing what is invisible demands our love for others in the form of creative attention. When we develop a school in a cultural bubble, our students lose out on the opportunities to learn to see the invisible. As a result, things that matter to others become truly invisible to our students. We are called to teach our students to pursue cross-bearing lives of sacrifice, service to others, and true worship to God; this ultimately is how we teach them to love all that God has created deeply.

In doing so, we need to ask ourselves if we have the love to pay creative attention to the voiceless, vulnerable, and invisible members in our community, the humility to enter into difficult diversity conversations, and the courage to actually do something about it even when we don't have everything figured out. We remember that God calls us to deconstruct our lives—Paul says to live is to die, and to die is to gain! (Philippians 1:21)—and He also calls us to lay down our lives for one another (John 15:13). In moving from "White to Mosaic," this means that we also lay down our privileges and self-centered priorities and enter into a shared endeavor to build a diverse community with a common cause, together.

Questions for Discussion

1. To what degree do you observe divided cultures in your classrooms and school community? What examples can you

---

5. Simone Weil, *Waiting for God* (New York: Harper Perennial Modern Classics, 2009), 149.

give of what you've observed?

2. How do you personally think about diversity in the Christian school? How might your thinking be similar or different to the perspectives of your colleagues? What are the implications of the Christian worldview for framing how we think about diversity?

3. Do honest conversations about race, privilege, and injustice happen at your school? If so, how are they received by all members of the community (students, teachers, leaders, parents)? If they do not happen now, how do you imagine community members would respond if invited into such conversations?

4. What inspired or challenged you from the three school stories—Prestonwood Christian Academy, The City School, and Boston Trinity Academy—that were shared in this chapter?

5. What needs to happen in your classroom and school for a more intentional and collaborative approach to creating a diverse, just, and authentic community? What resources might be available to you, both inside and outside of your school, to help foster that collaborative approach?

From Gutenberg to 5G

Mitchell Salerno and Keri D. Ingraham

In October 1517, Martin Luther nailed the *Disputation on the Power of Indulgences*, also known as the *Ninety-Five Theses*, on the door of the Castle Church in Wittenberg, Germany. Within a few months, Luther's written words were translated into German and printed for mass distribution. In a rather short period of time, his ideas spread across Europe, transforming the ecclesiastical world. Luther's influence placed him as a key leader during his era, and he remains known today due to his impact on the church and Western world.[1]

However, prior to Luther in early 15th century, Jan Hus (alternatively called John Hus, John Huss, Iohannes Hus, and Johannes Hus) preached and taught at Bethlehem Chapel in Prague. Hus adamantly preached against perceived injustices in the Roman Catholic Church. He was particularly disturbed by the sale of indulgences to finance the Pope's personal projects and wars.[2] Hus

---

1. "Martin Luther and the Printing Press," *Infoage*, 29 (Sept. 2011), accessed May 19, 2019, http://patrickkramer.umwblogs.org/2011/09/29/martin-luther-and-the-printing-press/.

2. "John Huss: Pre-Reformation Reformers," *Christian History: Learn the History of Christianity & the Church*, Christian History, 8 (Aug. 2008), accessed May 19, 2019, www.christianitytoday.com/history/people/martyrs/john-huss.html.

was a forerunner of the Reformation.[3] His thinking and teaching pre-date Luther by more than a century, yet Hus is unknown by most people.

Why is Luther the father of the Reformation while Hus has been largely forgotten? A key reason is Johannes Gutenberg's invention of the printing press around 1440—which was 25 years after Hus was burned at the stake. The printing press allowed Luther's ideas to be distributed quickly, widely, and cheaply. Hus lacked the connectivity of the mass-produced printed word. We're left to wonder how history might have been different if Hus had access to a more innovative means for distribution and connectivity as Luther did, thanks to Gutenberg's printing press.

It is undeniable that our current time period is marked by an explosion of innovation, which is transforming the way we live, connect, and communicate. This chapter will consider the transition from Gutenberg to Google—and to the 5G future just on the horizon—and implications for our Christian school context in the 21st century.

From Gutenberg to Google… and 5G

Gutenberg's invention of movable type, better known as the printing press, has been considered the greatest invention in history: "The historical breakthrough and subsequent cultural revolution occurred when Gutenberg reproduced a full Bible….What once took a monastic scribe two years to reproduce by hand was achieved in two weeks by the printing press—a 98 percent reduction in time and cost."[4] The printing press revolutionized society as information could be shared more quickly than before and in larger volume. This distribution of information led to the Reformation and the Enlightenment.

---

3. Trevor O'Reggio, "John Huss and the Origins of the Protestant Reformation," *Journal of the Adventist Theological Society* 28, no. 2, Article 6 (2017), accessed May 19, 2019, https://digitalcommons.andrews.edu/jats/vol28/iss2/6/.

4. Rex Miller, Bill Latham, and Brian Cahill, *Humanizing the Education Machine: How to Create Schools That Turn Disengaged Kids into Inspired Learners* (Hoboken, NJ: John Wiley & Sons, 2017), 61.

This powerful lever for distributing information in the 1400s can be compared with the modern world's information on demand through the World Wide Web, and more specifically, the ever-popular search engine, Google. With the typing of a few words, or even mere letters, information is instantly available and in vast quantity. It is rare that a word, phrase, or question entered into Google's search bar returns void of information. According to Rex Miller, "The current Google revolution is having a chaotic, conflictive, and disruptive effect that is similar to Gutenberg's printing press, multiplied across the globe."[5] The impact on day-to-day life for those with internet access has transformed the public square and marketplace.

But Google is just the beginning. Over the coming years, we will transition from a hodgepodge collection of local Wi-Fi and cellular networks, to a new super-network called 5th Generation, or 5G. 5G is approximately 100 times faster than the current fastest LTE (4G) network, which will make connectivity and data transfer nearly instantaneous.[6] More importantly, 5G will become the foundation for the future, supporting innovation and propelling technology forward in exponential ways. The promise of 5G is nothing less than turning science fiction into reality.

5G will become the foundation for the future, supporting innovation and propelling technology forward in exponential ways. The promise of 5G is nothing less than turning science fiction into reality.

Artificial intelligence (AI) is just one example. For AI to work properly, it requires a substantially faster network than we currently have, which 5G will provide. In his book, *Rewiring Education: How Technology Can Unlock Every Student's Potential*, John Couch, Apple's first vice president of education, explains, "Artificial intelligence is computer software with the ability to do things that can typically

---

5. Ibid., 62.

6. Paul-Christian Britz, "What Is 5G and Why Do We Care?" DW (November 26, 2018), accessed April 6, 2019, https://www.dw.com/en/what-is-5g-and-why-do-we-care/a-46456806.

only be done through human intelligence, such as problem solving, decision making, and complex voice and visual translations…. If there's one technology with *unlimited* potential, it's AI, because as computers begin to learn, think, and adapt by themselves, there really will be no more ceiling on possibility."[7]

What will this look like for schools? Thanks to AI, a school in Hangzhou, China, has experimented with facial recognition for the purpose of taking attendance and, more importantly, attempting to monitor student learning engagement.[8] This is fascinating and perhaps a bit frightening. Taking attendance, monitoring engagement, and assessing students has traditionally been the responsibility of the classroom teacher. But there's potential here as well: if AI can complete managerial tasks with accuracy and efficiency, it can free teachers to focus more on the human element of teaching, such as developing the student-teacher relationship.

We are educating students to live, work, and thrive in tomorrow's world, not today's (and definitely not the world of yesterday, in which we grew up).

The school in China is only the beginning. What will become of foreign language requirements in schools, when 5G enables AI to instantaneously translate verbal communication between people speaking different languages, which is under development right now?[9]

What will happen to student engagement when mixed reality (MR)—a combination of virtual reality (VR) and augmented

---

7. John D. Couch and Jason Towne, *Rewiring Education: How Technology Can Unlock Every Student's Potential* (Dallas, TX: BenBella Books, 2018), 190.

8. "China 'Intelligent Classroom Behavior Management System' Facial Recognition (Techjuice)," YouTube video, 1:14, posted by "DN," May 27, 2018, https://www.youtube.com/watch?v=k39oR2fLFPg.

9. Agence France-Presse, "CES 2019: Real-Time Translation Devices Step Closer to Reality at CES," *Gadgets 360* (January 11, 2019), accessed April 6, 2019, https://gadgets.ndtv.com/tv/features/ces-2019-real-time-translation-devices-step-closer-to-reality-at-1975667.

reality (AR) technologies[10]—allows them to gather virtually for real-time instruction in a virtual classroom with students from all over the globe (think holograms and avatars)? What will school administrators do when blockchain, a system that publicly records and stores transactions, streamlines and automates how we handle student records, transcript management, student identity management, library management, business operations, and much more?[11]

One more example of the technological revolution that is at our doorstep is what Couch and others call "The Internet of Things (IoT)," or "technology like integrated circuits, electronics, sensors, software, and so forth that's embedded directly into common everyday items like clothes, appliances, cars, furniture, utensils, and just about everything else."[12] We can see glimpses of what lies ahead with today's internet-enabled refrigerators, home security systems, and cleaning robots. But the coming IoT means that almost everything students and teachers touch, wear, hold, sit on, and pass by will soon be seamlessly connected to the Internet. We can forget struggling to manage students' cell phones in the classrooms—and in fact, some suggest forgetting cell phones altogether, as they become obsolete in a 24-7, 360-degree environment that is completely touch- and voice-enabled, all thanks to 5G.

Implications for Christian Education

As we consider this almost unfathomable progress, it is important to remember we are educating students to live, work, and thrive in tomorrow's world, not today's (and definitely not the world of yesterday, in which we grew up). Today's schools need to prepare students for a world that none of us have yet seen or experienced. For

---

10. Couch and Towne, *Rewiring Education*, 205.

11. Tom Vander Ark, "20 Ways Blockchain Will Transform (Okay, May Improve) Education," *Forbes* (August 20, 2018), accessed April 6, 2019, https://www.forbes.com/sites/tomvanderark/2018/08/20/26-ways-blockchain-will-transform-ok-may-improve-education/#29f6e46e4ac9.

12. Couch and Towne, *Rewiring Education*, 194.

example, Duke University professor Cathy Davidson predicts that 65% of students in elementary school will hold jobs that have yet to be created,[13] and according to futurist Thomas Frey, approximately 50% of jobs in our current world will not exist by the year 2030.[14] Each of these innovations will soon be not only commonplace, but also instrumental in preparing students for the era in which they live.[15]

Without question, technology is fraught with risk, and it's healthy to have a sense of apprehension about the dangers of a 5G future and what it means for human flourishing. Christian educators in particular need to consider how to leverage technology with care and intentionality, in ways that advance—and do not detract from—their schools' missions. We contend that a 5G world offers us unprecedented opportunities in three key areas: enhancing student engagement and learning; expanding access to Christian education; and re-clarifying our focus as Christ-centered schools.

Enhancing Student Engagement and Learning

Technology in schools is nothing new. Looking back, we see that in 1981, on average, there was one computer for every 125 students.[16] Ten years later in 1991, the ratio was one to 18. In

---

13. Mike Ettling, "How To Attract Talent For Jobs That Don't Exist Yet," *Forbes* (October 13, 2015), accessed April 07, 2019, https://www.forbes.com/sites/sap/2015/10/13/how-to-attract-talent-for-jobs-that-dont-yet-exist/#3ff2b5a37726.

14. Ibid.

15. Omar Abbosh and Larry Downes, "5G's Potential, and Why Businesses Should Start Preparing for It," *Harvard Business Review* (March 5, 2019): accessed April 6, 2019, https://hbr.org/2019/03/5gs-potential-and-why-businesses-should-start-preparing-for-it.

16. Damian Maher, Renata Phelps, Nikkita Urane, and Mal Lee, "Primary School Teachers' Use of Digital Resources with Interactive Whiteboards: The Australian Context," *Australasian Journal of Educational Technology* 28, no. 1 (2012): 138-58, accessed May 19, 2019, https://eric.ed.gov/?id=EJ976017.

2009, the ratio was one to five,[17] and since then schools are moving rapidly toward one-to-one learning. Many schools have gone a step further by implementing blended and/or online learning. But does an internet-connected device in the hands of a teacher and/or a student automatically bring about authentic and meaningful student learning? The answer, of course, is no.

When the first-generation iPad went on the market in April 2010, Monte Vista Christian School (MVCS)—located in Silicon Valley—became one of the first schools in the country to utilize iPads in the classroom. Since then, MVCS has remained an early adopter of technology but has done so in an intentional and ongoing effort to transform the school environment and pedagogy. For example, students no longer carry textbooks or need a locker for book storage, because they are encouraged to use technology to take initiative in their learning and create (rather than merely memorize and recite information). Classroom and office spaces have been redesigned to be flexible, in order to encourage and promote collaboration between faculty and students and between leaders and faculty.

Effective use of technology to enhance student engagement and learning does not happen by accident or default.

In its ongoing journey toward effective technology implementation and innovative pedagogy, MVCS has not abandoned its mission or thrown traditional ways of learning out the window. Instead, leaders and faculty have adopted a mindset of continual reflection and growth, where they consistently ask how technology can help the school better fulfill its mission and enhance student learning. For example, higher levels of comfort with digital content enabled MVCS to implement project-based learning in 2013, where students and teachers in grades 6-8 collaborate, design, and problem solve. In

---

17. Lucinda Gray, Nina Thomas, and Laurie Lewis, *Teachers' Use of Educational Technology in U.S. Public Schools: 2009,* (Washington DC: National Center for Education Statistics, Institute of Education Sciences, US Department of Education, 2010), accessed April 7, 2019, https://nces.ed.gov/pubs2010/2010040.pdf.

this example, the proliferation and regular use of internet-connected devices led to an increase in student exploration and authentic learning.

Effective use of technology to enhance student engagement and learning does not happen by accident or default. In our experiences in leading technological change in education, we have found the SAMR model[18] to provide a useful framework. The SAMR model has four levels, and technology has increasing value when moving beyond the first level of the SAMR Model to higher levels. The lowest level of the SAMR Model is called *substitution*, in which technology simply replaces what was completed without electronic technology previously; for example, a document is provided electronically instead of via hard copy to students. The next level is *augmentation*, where technology serves as an effective tool that enhances student engagement or provides immediate feedback, thereby improving pedagogy. *Modification* is the third level, in which technology is utilized to transform classroom learning tasks, such as adding an audio component to students' written work. The highest level is called *redefinition*, which allows for new learning that is not possible without the technology tool. An example of redefinition would be students exploring a geographical location with Google Earth, instead of simply reading about it or watching a video filmed in that location; in this example, technology allows students to have a first-hand look and navigate their own unique exploration of anywhere in the world, which fundamentally redefines their learning.

Throughout history, the message of Christ has been proclaimed with all available innovative tools—and today's Christian schools should be no different.

The promises of a 5G world for reaching this highest level—for redefining learning—is nothing short of astounding. Using this last example, imagine that instead of using Google Earth, 5G-enabled classrooms allow students to utilize VR and AR to experience another

18. Ruben Puentedura, "SAMR Model," *Technology Is Learning,* accessed April 13, 2019, https://sites.google.com/a/msad60.org/technology-is-learning/samr-model.

geographical setting or time period firsthand. They can even join up with students from across the state or around the world to explore a virtual world together. Moreover, they can collaborate in this dynamic and interactive environment, to develop and test solutions in conditions that closely resemble those in the real world. Imagine what this technology will mean for learning and engagement, as students virtually and collaboratively conduct scientific experiments, work on engineering projects, and study archeological digs or historical events.

Of course, the big question that every teacher and leader must ask is whether our schools and classrooms are ready for the 5G educational world. And readiness means both technologically and pedagogically: we need to be prepared not only in terms of providing the technology to facilitate a redefinition of learning, but also in terms of our understanding of how to engage students successfully in this new approach to learning.

Expanding Access to Christian Education

The market reality for private schools, including Christian schools, has become increasingly challenging in recent years—due to a financial model based almost exclusively on consumers' ability and willingness to pay high tuition rates. This has been exacerbated by technological advances in the marketplace, where online search engines provide on-demand consumer choice regardless of geographical location to the vendor. This has made the educational marketplace more competitive, with the consumer playing a larger, more powerful role than perhaps witnessed in history. The impact of e-commerce and a la carte pricing cannot be underestimated as it relates to private schooling.

In response, Prestonwood Christian Academy launched PCA*plus* as part of its system of schools in 2009. PCA*plus* leverages technology to offer students in grades 6-12 innovative opportunities to complete coursework and work toward a diploma, while meeting consumer demand for a lower price point. PCA*plus* achieves this through three distinct offerings: allowing homeschool students the opportunity to take courses on campus; providing online students the chance to earn credits and/or a diploma through an accredited virtual academy; and enabling students to craft a customized hybrid schedule of both on-campus and online courses, in an a la carte model.

These three options have enabled the school to create a more flexible financial model, by filling empty seats in its brick and mortar classrooms, providing a creative revenue stream while not increasing fixed costs, and expanding the school's reach by allowing the consumer to pick the individual course(s) desired at a la carte pricing—instead of a one-size-fits-all, full-time brick and mortar single offering, at a comprehensive high dollar price point. And missionally, this flexible model has resulted in Christian education becoming viable to a wider market not only because of increased financial accessibility, but also because of reaching new populations (whether those with learning differences, athletes or others who require more flexible learning schedules, or those who are sick or injured). Similarly, connectivity has been expanded from the small geographical radius of the school's physical location, to provide accessibility around the world with asynchronous online courses.

Christian schools need to develop new, sustainable business models that leverage technology and innovation to respond to today's rapidly changing, competitive educational market. It would be short-sighted, however, to view this simply in terms of enabling Christian schools to improve their viability. The reality is that Christian education is simply not reaching all of the students whose families wish to access it—often due to finances. Ultimately, leveraging technology to expand access to Christ-centered education means greater missional reach for Christian schools.

Re-Clarifying Our Focus

This leads us to a final consideration when it comes to the consequences of a 5G world for Christian education. We've seen that technology, when properly leveraged, can help us to better engage students in learning and provide greater access to Christ-centered education. But perhaps most importantly, the technology-driven changes that are coming can drive us to clarify our focus in Christian education.

Clearly, a highly connected and digital world requires thoughtful and discerning leadership related to student safety, monitoring, and accountability measures. Without question, students must be taught the appropriate use of technology. But instead of just policies, rules, and regulations, becoming a Christ-honoring user of technology happens best in the context of meaningful student-teacher relationships—which are characterized by trust, open communication, and modeling. The influence of technology in our students' lives gives us an opportunity to engage them in the discipleship work of Colossians 1:28, as Paul writes: "Him we proclaim, warning everyone and teaching everyone with all wisdom, that we may present everyone mature in Christ."

Finally, we must realize that throughout history, the message of Christ has been proclaimed with all available innovative tools—and today's Christian schools should be no different. Ready or not, the third education revolution is upon us.[19] The days of Gutenberg and even Google will soon be in the past, as we enter a 5G world. Technology can and ought to be leveraged to impact students, their families, and our communities more effectively, moving them to increased love, devotion, and knowledge of God, while also expanding accessibility to reach more students with the hope of Christ through Christian education.

Questions for Discussion

1. How do you articulate your personal vision for technology in Christian schools and classrooms, and what variance might there be among your colleagues in your school?

2. To what extent does your school employ technology to enhance its pursuit of outcomes? How are you measuring the effectiveness of your efforts?

---

19. Donna Orem, "How the Third Education Revolution Is Shifting Our Approach to Learning," *National Association of Independent Schools Magazine*, (Spring 2019), accessed April 6, 2019, https://www.nais.org/magazine/independent-school/spring-2019/how-the-third-education-revolution-is-shifting-our-approach-to-learning/.

3. What do you think the impact of 5G and technologies it will enable (AR, VR, IoT) will have on education? What impact might it have on your own students and school?

4. What excites you about the future of technology in education? What concerns you?

5. What impact does technology have on the way students relate with one another and develop their identity?

6. How might schools in the future be physically set up if technological impacts continue to accelerate as predicted? How might that impact or transform the concept of a school as a community?

7. How can you work with colleagues, students, and families to align technology with a Christian worldview, and leverage it to better fulfill your school's mission?

From Siloed to Engaged

Daniel Pampuch and Darren Iselin

The Farming Silo

As you drive through the rich rural heartlands of Australia, you will encounter large grain silos that tower like skyscrapers above the otherwise flat and predictable fertile plains. They are a feature of the landscape and serve as landmarks for the local communities and an essential part of farming life.

Silos are used by farming communities to store grain for future use, for transport to a processing plant, or for export. They are a way of preserving what has been harvested and collected for future use or sale. Silos are also used to store grain for animals to supplement their diet and to provide much needed sustenance when fields are barren from drought or seasonal change.

In the same way that silos represent a level of technological advancement and success for the farmer, departments in organizations, businesses, and schools represent a level of capacity, specialization and professional capability. To say one can call on the IT department, or refer an issue to HR, is often considered the hallmark of an organization that has reached maturity and scale. Silos in the workplace have been used to establish boundaries, maintain order, and allow teams to operate in focused and specialized ways.

During times of stability and growth, the positives of silos may outweigh the negatives. Yet during times of significant change, when organizations must be agile, silos can be stubborn obstacles to creating a more effective path to growth and sustainability. Furthermore, in the cultural landscapes that confront schools and educational organizations, silos impede rather than cultivate a shared purpose and vision for the school community.

In our "Christian educational settings, silos become impediments to flexibility, adaptability, and engagement to produce synergy."[1] According to Lencioni, silos are nothing more than the barriers that exist between departments within an organization, thereby causing people who are supposed to be on the same team to work against one another.[2] Lencioni states, "Silos—and the turf wars they enable—devastate organizations. They waste resources, kill productivity, and jeopardize the achievement of goals."[3]

For the Christian school, breaking down silos is a biblical principle.

Challenging the Siloed Model

The old top-down structures of organizations are mechanistic in form and design. This makes them highly susceptible to challenges in times of unpredictability, or when confronted by disruptive change.[4] According to McKinsey,[5] four disruptive trends are challenging the siloed nature of many organizations:

---

1. Bryan Miller, "Silos to Synergy: A Necessary Shift," *ACSI Blog,* March 5, 2019, accessed March 25, 2019, https://blog.acsi.org/silos-to-synergy.

2. Patrick Lencioni, *Silos, Politics and Turf Wars: A Leadership Fable about Destroying the Barriers that Turn Colleagues into Competitors* (San Francisco: Jossey Bass, 2006), 175.

3. Ibid.

4. Steve Aronowitz, Aaron De Smet and Deirdre McGinty, "Getting Organizational Design Right," *McKinsey Quarterly* (June 2015): 1.

5. Wouter Aghina, Karin Ahlback, Aaron De Smet, Gerald Lackey, Michael Lurie, Monica Murarka, and Christopher Handscomb, "The Five Trademarks of Agile Organizations," *McKinsey Report* (June 2018): 4.

- Quickly evolving environments and conditions;
- Constant introduction of disruptive technology;
- Accelerating digitization and democratization of information; and
- The war for highly talented and skilled employees.

Each of these trends is familiar to Christian schools. Educational markets and student demographics are rapidly shifting, technology is reshaping daily how we engage students and families, and we face an alarming dearth of qualified next-generation leaders.[6]

These forces may be driving us to consider the need to challenge the siloed model, but it is important to consider that for the Christian school, breaking down silos is a biblical principle. Nothing captures the concept of silos better than the laws, traditions, and practices surrounding the life of the Pharisees, with hundreds of laws governing their daily lives. Pharisees painstakingly struggled to fulfill all of them, and rabbis provided guidance on how to navigate their application in society.

In Luke 10:25-37, Jesus is confronted by a lawyer about how he might fulfill the law and achieve eternal life. Jesus responds, "Love the Lord your God with all your heart, soul and strength and love your neighbor as yourself." "Who is my neighbor?" asks the lawyer to justify himself. In response, Jesus tell the story of the good Samaritan.

Samaritans customarily did not have dealings with Jews.[7] Safely considered the farthest from a modern-day "neighbor" in every regard, the Samaritan in the story both felt and showed compassion toward a beaten man. He used wine and oil, both expensive goods, to tend to the man's wounds. He took him to an inn, paid two days' salary for his care, and offered to pay more as needed with no assurance of receiving anything in return. Beyond material contribution, the Samaritan gave up his own comfort, resigning to walk to the inn, carrying the injured man on his animal.

---

6. Daniel Pampuch, "Making Way for Millennials in Leadership," *ACSI Blog* (Jun 26, 2018), accessed April 14, 2019, https://blog.acsi.org/making-way-millennials-leadership.

7. Mishna Shebiith 8:10, accessed March 25, 2019, https://halakhah.com/pdf/zeraim/Sheviith.pdf.

He also forfeited his anonymity by staying the night, thereby risking accusation by association and defilement.

What *compelled* the Samaritan to do something radically different from the norm? What was his vision for the world? For Greer and Horst, the proactive question Christian leaders need to ask themselves is this: "Are we more animated about building our own little clan or about building the kingdom of God?"[8] For them, the Kingdom is where we submit our efforts to God's reigning authority and become co-laborers in a shared mission to bring heaven to earth.[9] Bruno and Dirks claim that active gospel-centered partnership can only be marked by one driving passion: The Kingdom.[10] Bearing the name of Christ, Christian schools ought to be places known for ministry marked by mutual submission, shared purpose, and gospel-mindedness, and not by the isolation, disengagement, or competitiveness that are characteristics of siloed organizations.

Moving from Siloed to Engaged

Silos arise not because of what we are doing wrong but rather because of what we are failing to do. First, we fail to provide employees with a compelling context for working together. Without a compelling context, employees at all levels are easily side-tracked, moving in different directions, often at cross purposes.[11] We also fail to provide work structures that would facilitate that compelling context by fostering meaningful collaboration among employees toward shared goals. And ultimately, every departmental silo in any organization can be traced back to its leaders, who have failed to understand the interdependencies that must exist among the leadership team, or who have failed to make those interdependencies clear to people deeper in

---

8. Peter Greer and Chris Horst, *Rooting for Rivals: How Collaboration and Generosity Increase the Impact of Leaders, Charities and Churches* (Bloomington, MN: Bethany House, 2018), 51.

9. Ibid, 64.

10. Chris Bruno and Matt Dirks, *Churches Partnering Together: Biblical Strategies, for Fellowship, Evangelism and Compassion* (Wheaton, Il: Crossway, 2014), 41.

11. Lencioni, *Silos, Politics and Turf Wars,* 176.

their own departments.[12]

We are convicted by Scripture and compelled by disruptive change in education that organizational silos must give way to genuine engagement in common purpose and missional work. The question is, how?

To this end, all organizations in all industries and sectors are moving from rigid structures to more agile and organic forms similar to that of "organisms."[13] In such models, discrete structures and lines of accountability are replaced by teams and inter-departmental working groups. Leaders provide overall direction and release the necessary resources for teams to develop effective and timely solutions.[14] This integrated "organic" model is characterized by four key elements: *strategy*, *structure*, *process*, and *people*.

Strategy is the single most important element of the integrated model and must be embodied across the organization. Employees at all levels need to share the same vision and purpose for the organization, which drives them to sense and seize opportunities to fulfil this mission when they arise. Organizational leaders move from a position of command and control to one of freeing-up the necessary resources and expertise and providing timely strategic guidance.[15]

Bearing the name of Christ, Christian schools ought to be places known for ministry marked by mutual submission, shared purpose, and gospel-mindedness, and not by the isolation, disengagement, or competitiveness that are characteristics of siloed organizations.

In regard to *structure*, departments or centers are replaced by

---

12. Ibid., 177.

13. Gareth Morgan, *Images of Organization* (Beverly Hills: Sage Publications, 1986).

14. Aronowitz, De Smet and McGinty, "Getting Organizational Design Right," 6.

15. Aghina, et. al, "The Five Trademarks of Agile Organizations," 8.

a network of empowered teams. Such dynamic teams are flat and have clearly defined roles. Teams are seen as robust communities of practice with active partnerships across the organization.[16]

Such a grass-roots level approach allows for a *process* of both rapid decision-making and learning cycles to occur. Standardized approaches to work are replaced by rapid iteration and experimentation.[17] In an environment characterized by information transparency, continuous learning and action-oriented decision-making is favored.[18]

"Students don't just come to learn information; they come to be part of an authentic community—perhaps for the first time in their lives they are experiencing community—and we must not be disconnected, selfish nor insular in our response to this longing of their hearts."

From separated silos of specialization, the school moves to a dynamic *people* model that ignites passion. As members of teams from across the organization are mobilized in the same direction, the result is a cohesive community with entrepreneurial drive. As roles become mobile, to see the end achieved, traditional hierarchies of leadership are replaced by shared and servant leadership styles.

Shalom in Action: Considering Who is My Neighbor

The following vignette recounts the remarkable journey of a Christian school in Australia and seeks to showcase what one school can do when it takes seriously the question "Who is my neighbor?" It also illustrates how a compelling vision of authentic community and

16. Wouter Aghina, Aaron De Smet and Kristen Weerda, "Agility: It Rhymes with Stability," *McKinsey Quarterly* (December 2015), 4-6.

17. Gary P. Pisano, "The Hard Truth About Innovative Cultures," *Harvard Business Review* (Jan-Feb 2019), 65.

18. Wouter, De Smet and Weerda, "Agility: It Rhymes with Stability," 10-11.

organic networks transforms a community with united purpose, strategy, and direction.

The intentional breaking down of a siloed organization into a well-functioning organism is exemplified in the transformation of Shalom College[19], which is a thriving K-12 school community of over 1500 students, located near the agricultural "granite belt" in Queensland, Australia. While student enrollment had been steady since inception, organizational functionality had incrementally and somewhat insidiously established clearly defined silos with the school's culture.

In 2012, a new principal, Mark Francis, was appointed[20], and over the next seven years he and his team undertook a transformative journey that re-imagined a functional but siloed school faculty into a thriving, engaged, and seamlessly integrated school community. Significantly, their inspiring story of moving from siloed to engaged is not just an internal transformation within staff faculty and systems; it is also a celebration of the transformation Shalom has experienced with their wider neighborhood and community. The remainder of this chapter will lay out five key tenets that guided Shalom's transformation from a siloed to an engaged school community.

1. **We are compelled to act out of an inclusive and embodied vision that answers the question, "Who is my neighbor?"**

Upon his appointment at Shalom, Mark Francis spent his first 12 months defining the core elements of the Shalom College distinctive and vision. He was slow to act, preferring to listen intently to the voices, past and present, both from within the school setting and the wider community, as he deliberately sought to map the contours and cultural heartbeat of the school. Deliberate and sustained listening led to the formulation of a well-distilled yet succinct vision statement, a compelling "why" for change that would

---

19. Shalom College is a pseudonym. For readers outside of Australia, note that a "college" is a school which offers grades through high school; the term "university" is used to refer to a post-secondary institution.

20. Mark Francis is a pseudonym. For readers outside of Australia, "principal" is the title given to the head of school.

challenge and ultimately dismantle entrenched siloed behavior.

Mark and his leadership team were motivated by a passionate desire to embody and articulate an authentic Christian school community, whereby all members contributed in networked, relational, and cohesive ways of working and interacting. Mark was convinced Shalom needed to create authentic community at every level within the school—starting with leadership but flowing out to faculty, staff interactions, student engagement, and wider community involvement. He envisioned a "real" community that was not defined by the lines of demarcation, delegated power, or positional authority, but that was united in the central tenet of what it meant to be image-bearers serving other image-bearers in an authentic Christian community. As Mark explains, "Students don't just come to learn information; they come to be part of an authentic community—perhaps for the first time in their lives they are experiencing community—and we must not be disconnected, selfish nor insular in our response to this longing of their hearts."[21]

To enact this community, the Shalom team set about embodying, reinforcing and reiterating three simple yet non-negotiable core values—*belonging*, *learning*, and *community* underpinned by the Gospel—throughout the entire staff. Decision-making became less reactive and far more intentional, through the repeated use of a guiding question: *Will this decision help staff and students belong, assist with staff and students' learning, and promote and celebrate community both within the school and across the wider community?* Through this simplified and reframed discourse, applied consistently, Shalom was defining and delineating who their neighbors were—and what implications their actions, behavior, attitudes, and ways of working and interacting would have upon their neighbors. Slowly, the silos within faculties, the silos within staff rooms, the silos within classrooms, and the silos between leadership and teachers began to break down. Interestingly, as these silos began to dissipate, so too did the silos across the community—between teachers and parents, between students and teachers, and between school and neighborhood.

---

21. Interview with "Mark Francis" conducted by author, March 6, 2019.

2. We intentionally come into orbit and proximity with those with whom we do not normally associate or cooperate.

As the shared vision became known and embodied throughout the Shalom community, seeds of collaboration and newly formed partnerships began to emerge. These new ways of working and relating stressed the importance of relational proximity when working with others and for others. A service orientation began to become the preferred mode of working within the Shalom community, as staff were no longer merely about serving out of self-interest or promotion of their own faculty or area. Rather than working in delineated and separate structures, teams began to emerge and work more intentionally together on a range of school-wide projects and initiatives.

For most staff this was a process of moving outside of their comfort zones and preconceived ways of doing things. This was not without suspicion or awkward adjustments, and in some cases, certain staff could not support these new modes of working more intentionally together. Some pockets of the community refused to work together and defiantly endeavoured to maintain the status quo. This required courageous decision-making by Mark and his leadership group. Shalom's leadership team kept these staff accountable and reminded them repeatedly of how every staff member and student at Shalom needed to embody this new way of working and relating. Inevitably, a small number of resisting staff chose to leave and were then replaced with those who embraced the vision.

Rather than passing by on the other side (Luke 23), staff began to break down these long-established modes of working in isolation. Divides between primary and secondary divisions were first confronted, and then staff began to actively seek out those with whom collaboration and partnership were not common. For example, industrial shop teachers began to host "Boys Without Dads" days for primary students, with remarkable results. Teachers in the school's hospitality department began breakfast clubs for the entire school community. If there were no active supports or facilitation of structures to assist these fledgling programs and the significant buy-in of leadership, staff and students, the flourishing of these new shoots of opportunity may not have ever taken root.

3. **We actively remove the suspicion of the "other" and replace it with a network of the "known."**

As the once well-established silos began to be deconstructed, the Shalom community intentionally sought to remove the suspicion of "the other" by promoting and consistently celebrating the networks of the "known." Such intentionality necessitated the deconstruction of a range of alternate narratives that had arisen due to working in isolation. Silo myths were confronted and then re-storied around the new narrative of working in empowered networked teams at Shalom.

The greatest of these was what Mark Francis referred to as the "the myth of an executive." To overcome a siloed workplace, Mark realized that the modelling of collaboration must occur at the top. A suspicion of senior leadership as being disconnected from the rest of the school community was acknowledged and confronted. Leadership needed to model what being self-reflective and transparent looked like to staff. The leadership group was reimagined and restructured to ensure that there was an embodiment of an engaged and integrated vision. Shalom developed a "no executive'" policy—and a new narrative was established that viewed all in senior leadership as "teachers who happen to hold leadership roles." Such a subtle yet dramatic change in perception was far-reaching and established great currency regarding trust and credibility of the new leadership team. Visibility of the leadership team became a priority, and the leadership team was highly intentional about coming into the orbit of teaching staff and students. Such servant-oriented leadership—image-bearers serving image-bearers—impacted staff deeply and modeled a better way of doing community for the entire school.

This approach extended from the internal community of the school to the external. To develop a network of the "known" with the larger community, Shalom had to develop new language that was both redefined and reinforced as authentic and inclusive. Mark Francis explained, "Often church language is judgemental, hypocritical, never wrong, rulemaking. The community of Shalom in contrast wanted to be a safe place—the church's new front door—real and authentic."[22] This new language of communicating to parents of a largely non-Christian clientele helped break down the internal/external silos existing between Shalom College and its local community.

4. **The Word became flesh and blood and moved into the neighborhood.**

As new ways of serving and working became normalized, a plethora of newly-imagined projects and initiatives began to be birthed. These projects were diverse in their scope and inclusive and collaborative in their involvement, necessitating teams that consisted of staff from across the school. For example:

- A community-oriented sports program, with a mission to grow both athletes and community, became so popular it required a diverse range of staff from across the entire college. As it continued to flourish (over 200 teams across five sports), the wider community embraced the concept that quickly spread to numerous schools in the region.
- A no-cost breakfast club was established but quickly grew to require student and staff volunteers from across the college; the club now serves over 400 students each day and is deeply valued and appreciated by the Shalom community.
- The annual school festival also was transformed due to the new modes of networked engagement and a commitment to belong in community; no longer a showcase of Shalom, it became a celebration of the local community. The entire community now works collaboratively together on this event, which has become a highlight in the calendar of the local region and attracts up to a staggering 10,000 visitors annually.

Such agile and action-oriented projects as these (and many others) enabled meaningful engagement and connection across the

---

22. Interview with "Mark Francis" conducted by author, March 6, 2019.

school community and further contributed to the eradication of silos within the Shalom College context.

A new narrative became established relating to serving the neighborhood through creating a sense of belonging and learning. The service and servant-orientated heart of the school now became the renewed soul of their community. This was no better demonstrated than in the hub around which so much of the Shalom community now revolves—Carey's Café. From humble beginnings in 2015 as a trade training center and a simple cake and coffee meeting place run by the hospitality department, the seed of this collaborative project has now become the fulcrum around which the entire Shalom community functions. Today, Carey's Café is a thriving center not only for food, but also for community-building. It has attracted broad community appeal, including five-dollar roast dinner days that are loved by adjacent nursing home residents, families, play groups, students, teachers, leaders, and all within the community. Mark Francis remarks that Carey's "talks and acts like a local—so that by any means the Gospel practically moves into the neighborhood—and we can celebrate together over food."[23]

The soul of Shalom's engaged, collaborative, networked and integrated model of community finds its fullest and most incarnational expression at Carey's. As Mark explains, "Carey's hasn't actually transformed things—but it has been the vehicle for the transformation to find expression."

5.   We demonstrate and celebrate faithful presence over time.

This transformation did not happen instantly nor without bold convictions regarding what a preferred and agile model of community and staff collaboration might look like. Courageous leadership inevitably did break and dispense with silos, but it took extended time of sustained obedience and an unwavering commitment to faithfully embody the vision and core values across

---

23. Interview with "Mark Francis" conducted by author, March 6, 2019.

this school community. Faithful presence[24] was required by faithful and dedicated people.

Mark speaks of the land that Shalom is built upon as being purposed by a faithful God: "Before the foundation of the world, God has set apart this land for education at this time in this place. In this way, God is sovereign, and this community is His instrument for serving this local place. To have an impact, you need to stay—stay for a long time. I'm here living 400 meters from school Monday to Friday doing community—investing in this place and being rooted—living like a local, acting like a local, celebrating like a local."[25]

Mark and his team from Shalom have remained faithful over years. Moving from silos to engaged is not an act—it is a process. Over time, the seeds that were once held in demarcated silos have been given opportunity to be planted, nurtured, and nourished. Now, in due season, Shalom is reaping a bountiful harvest in the good soil of an integrated and connected school culture. The promise of Galatians 6:9—that we will reap a harvest, if we do not give up in doing good—is for any Christian school that seeks to journey from isolated silos to the engagement of authentic Christian community.

Questions for Discussion

1. How do you answer the question, "Who is my neighbor?" when it comes to education and to the Christian school? Might different types of answers exist within your own school and for your colleagues, and if so, what might they be?

2. What does community mean to you in your school, and what would living well together look and feel like?

3. Who are the outsiders in your school? How do your actions as a leader reinforce their position outside or welcome them in to community?

---

24. James Davison Hunter, *To Change the World: The Irony, Tragedy, and Possibility of Christianity in the Late Modern World* (Oxford: Oxford University Press, 2010).

25. Interview with "Mark Francis" conducted by author, March 6, 2019.

4. What holds you or your school back from leaving silos behind, to engaging those not normally in your orbit?

5. What insights or inspiration did you take away from the story of Shalom in this chapter?

6. How can your school take steps toward being more faithfully present in your community? What resources do you have, and what barriers do you face, in making steps toward engagement?

From Fear to Hope

Lynn E. Swaner and Jay Ferguson

Trolls Under the Bridge

All of our students today know what a "troll" is: someone on the Internet who deliberately provokes disagreement, stirs up controversy, and aims to cause needless pain or harm. As educators, or even as parents, we're likely familiar with trolls from the old Norwegian folk tale *Billy Goats Gruff*. Three billy goats have to cross a bridge in the spring to get to a hillside so they can eat grass and fatten up. But there's a scary troll who lives under the bridge. Each time one of the goats walks over, the troll taunts it and threatens, "I'm going to gobble you up."

The first two goats manage to cross the bridge by convincing the troll to wait for the final goat, who is the largest and therefore promises to be the best meal. But when the third goat crosses the bridge, he's indeed big enough to battle the troll and destroy it.

As we stand on the precipice of the future of Christian education, it is abundantly clear that we need to build a bridge to the other side. This bridge needs to takes us from a scarcity to an abundance mindset; from a machine-like model of education to a humanized approach, aligned with how God created us to learn; from divided, dominant-cultural campuses to mosaic communities that are welcoming and inclusive; and from schools and departments that are siloed and isolated to ones that are fully engaged and networked. But, like this story, we have trolls already camped out under the bridge—even as it's being built!

Our "trolls" are those things that keep us up at night—fears, anxieties, distorted self-awareness that leads us to doubt our abilities to teach our students well or lead our people to be everything God calls them to be. These fears distract us from what God can do through us and restricts our vision to a myopic, reductionistic version of who we are and what God calls us to do.

In a recent exercise with a group of Christian education leaders, they were asked to identify the trolls under their bridge to the future, as well as what each is saying to them. Here are the trolls they described:

- Self-preservation… "Change will only lead to loss, and it means having to endure endings."
- Self-reliance… "We don't have the capacity to change."
- Inertia… "This is the way we've always done it."
- Nostalgia… "That's not how we used to do it in the golden years."
- Turfism… "This is *my* turf, so stay off!"
- Paralysis… "What if that isn't the right way?"
- Comfort… "It's all about what makes me personally comfortable."
- Prognostication… "We've tried that before and it didn't work… so it won't work this time either."
- Resignation… "Why bother? There's nothing new under the sun."
- Playing it safe… "If you try to solve this problem, you'll just create five new ones that are worse."
- Uncertainty… "There are lots of unknowns."
- Failure… "But what if it doesn't work?"

Each of these trolls can originate from a way of thinking, a structure or process, an attitude, or even an aspect of an organization's DNA. From a scriptural perspective, trolls can be principalities and powers against which we must wrestle (Ephesians 6:12). Regardless of where the troll comes from, its ultimate goal is to scare us—to make us put down our tools for building the bridge, turn around and go back the way we came, and ultimately ensure that we never reach the other side.

Put simply, trolls are fears that keep us from going where God has called us. And to be sure, there is power in simply naming the fears. We would encourage you to sit down with your colleagues and engage in this same exercise and see if you can put a face to the fears that may be keeping you from moving forward. But we can't stop there. Instead, as in the fable, we have to speak to the fear—and remind it that someone bigger is coming. For believers, that someone is, of course, Jesus. 1 John 4:4 tells us that, as God's children, "you are from God and have overcome them, for he who is in you is greater than who is in the world."

These fears distract us from what God can do through us and restricts our vision to a myopic, reductionistic version of who we are and what God calls us to do.

Along these lines, that same group of Christian educators who identified these fears also spent time sharing scriptural rebuttals: for nostalgia, they found 1 Thessalonians 4:10 NASB ("We urge you brothers, to excel still more") and Isaiah 43:18 ("Remember not the former things, nor consider the things of old"); to inertia, they cited Hebrews 11:8 ("By faith Abraham obeyed when he was called to go out to a place that he was to receive as an inheritance. And he went out, not knowing where he was going"); to self-reliance, they recalled Ephesians 3:20 ("to him who is able to do far more abundantly than all we ask or think, according to the power at work within us"); and so on.

This final step in the exercise was not merely quoting Scripture; instead, it was doing what 2 Corinthians 10:5 says we must do: "We destroy arguments and every lofty opinion raised against the knowledge of God, and take every thought captive to obey Christ." The goal is to bring our fears about change in Christian education into submission to truth through the love of God (1 John 4:18) and in doing so, begin to move toward hope.

Through the MindShift process and dialogues, we've come to recognize overcoming fear as the linchpin for embarking on all of the change journeys identified in MindShift. Fear will entrap us in a scarcity mindset, and fear will keep us in isolation from others. Fear will prevent us from the hard work of examining ourselves and trying to understand those we perceive as the "other." Fear will make us feel too small and powerless to humanize the machine at the root of our educational system, and fear will convince us we'll be crushed by the onslaught of technological change.

For nearly every hero we can call to mind, overcoming fear is the pivotal *internal* battle that sets the stage for the hero's victory in the *external* battle. Robinson Crusoe must first conquer the overwhelming despair of shipwrecked solitude before he can harness nature to survive. In the Academy Award-winning film *Black Panther*, T'Challa's greatest battle is not leading his people to overcome the lethal Killmonger, but to move past the internal stagnation of tradition embraced by his ancestors and lead his people into an era of cross-cultural engagement. Overcoming fear as the central issue in MindShift shouldn't surprise us, because in the hero's journey of "from...to," overcoming fear is almost always at the heart of the story.

The goal is to bring our fears about change in Christian education into submission to truth through the love of God (1 John 4:18) and in doing so, begin to move toward hope.

The Sum of All Fears

In a time of precipitous and unprecedented change, educators are being called upon to do more than perhaps ever before. Drawing upon our conversations with hundreds of Christian school teachers and leaders across the country, we tried to name many of the fears accompanying this change for Christian educators.

Collectively speaking, we're afraid of losing our historical institutions, or the way we've always done things, or our four-walled schools as we have always known them. We're afraid of becoming irrelevant—that what we are doing won't matter much longer into the future. We're afraid of uncertainty, of not knowing exactly what to do, of not having that one "best practice" that we know for sure works. We're afraid that our school's survival is dependent upon us.

We suspect that it's even deeper and darker than this. If we're honest, we're afraid of what all these consequences of failure mean for us, personally: the loss of esteem in the eyes of others; the potential failure of our institutions, which reflects directly upon us; losing our own security, whether through our work, or our position, or our standing in the community; or, perhaps even losing our sense of self-worth. Yes, these fears are carnal, but they go to the depths of who we are when we are our most vulnerable, our most *broken* selves. And ultimately, and likely because of these fears, we've become afraid of taking risks.

We're not alone. Jake Becker, head of school at The City School in Philadelphia, always tells his school's story through the lens of the parable of the talents (Matthew 25) where we read about a servant who "plays it safe" because he is afraid. Unlike the two other servants in the parable who invest the master's money and effectively double it, the third servant instead confesses, "Master, I knew you to be a hard man, reaping where you did not sow and gathering where you scattered no seed, *so I was afraid*, and I went and hid your talent in the ground. Here, you have what is yours" (v. 14, emphasis added). Preserving the status quo was this fear-driven servant's approach to self-preservation.

The master is unimpressed by the servant's road to nowhere, calling the servant "wicked," and instead promoting the other two servants who took a risk. He punished the one who was fearful and failed to invest wisely what the master had given him. In this parable we learn that there is no reward for playing it safe with what God has asked us to invest in faith.

As Christian educators, God has asked us to invest a number of talents wisely—whether our own talents, our students', or our families'. These include time, human abilities, finances, educational backgrounds, physical resources, and relationships. Given today's changing educational and cultural climate, here are a few "risky" investments we need to make with these talents:

- Re-envisioning our master schedules to accommodate collaborative or experiential learning opportunities for students.
- Embracing new technologies in and out of the classroom, as well as practicing thoughtful and intentional sabbaticals from those technologies to promote stillness and reflection.
- Partnering with other Christian schools, churches, or community organizations to work together toward common goals and to share resources.
- Changing admissions policies or financial aid practices to meet the needs of today's families more effectively, as well as to broaden access to Christian education for students of all backgrounds.
- Considering alternative sources of income beyond the traditional tuition and fundraising model.
- Entrusting teachers with greater responsibility for the instructional culture of the school, and empowering them through teacher-led professional development and peer observations.
- Allocating resources to serve students, families, and communities that have been traditionally underserved.
- Giving students more opportunity for voice and choice in their studies, as well as authentic leadership experiences.
- Reimagining long-held curricular and pedagogical practices to ensure those means of learning truly enhance, rather than harm students' and teachers' natures as image-bearers of God.
- Taking a more active role and positively engaging in our communities and government, through service as well as advocacy.
- Sunsetting legacy programs and practices in targeted ways, to create capacity to do something new that God is commissioning.

As Christian educators, we know we are investing our talents well when we reap a good return on that investment, which we gauge primarily through student learning and discipleship. A good return on investment also means that our leaders, teachers, and staff are flourishing, and that we have positive relationships with school families, churches, and our communities. If the sum of all fears is not taking risks, the sum of investing our talents is—taken all together— school cultures and classrooms that are healthy and thriving. As in the parable, these kinds of returns come by taking these risks and trusting God for the outcome—not by playing it safe, out of fear.

Moving Toward Hope

Moving from burying our talents because of fear—toward a willingness to invest those talents—requires that we reframe our fears in terms of hope. Fundamentally, an educator's optimism is planted in hope: the hope that the God who is good and is actively at work in all the affairs of man is actively involved at this very minute in the life of our schools; the hope that the God who created our teachers, children, and parents loves them all much more than we even have the capacity to do, and that He is incessantly plotting for their good and His glory; the hope that as Christian educators, if we are truly trusting, abiding, and resting in our all-powerful, always active, limitlessly loving God, we cannot ultimately fail beyond His power to save.

> *If the sum of all fears is not taking risks, the sum of investing our talents is— taken all together—school cultures and classrooms that are healthy and thriving.*

But how do we do the hard work of moving from fear to hope? Fundamentally, we agree with C.S. Lewis' assertion in *Mere Christianity*:

> Really great moral teachers never do introduce new moralities: it is quacks and cranks who do that…. The real job of every moral teacher is to keep on bringing us back, time after time, to the old simple principles which we are all so anxious not

to see; like bringing a horse back and back to the fence it has refused to jump or bringing a child back and back to the bit in its lesson that it wants to shirk.[1]

Thus, we want to bring ourselves back to two principles that will help us move from fear to hope. The first is that we are *called to love*. As believers, our hope is entirely founded in the truth of God's Word and what He says about fear and its antidote, which is His love. A powerful way to apply that antidote is found in our second principle, which is that we are *called to remember*. It is through the discipline of remembrance that we can magnify God's love in our lives and in doing so move from fear to hope.

Called to Love

We know from living in a fallen world that fear is normal and natural. Genesis 3:10 records the first moment of fear experienced by humans in Adam's explanation of his and Eve's actions to hide from God: "I heard the sound of you in the garden, *and I was afraid*, because I was naked" (emphasis added). But while fear may be normal and natural, we also know from the Word of God that fear is not of the Spirit (2 Timothy 1:7).

Rather, our hope of defeating fear is rooted in the love of Jesus—it is hope rooted in perfect love. And, as the Apostle John reminds us, "There is no fear in love, but perfect love casts out fear. For fear has to do with punishment, and whoever fears has not been perfected in love" (I John 4:18). Freedom from fear is our birthright as children of the King, as His beloved in whom He is well pleased. We not only have to remember this simple, yet deeply profound truth, but also must keep it constantly before ourselves, our colleagues, and our students.

It is not enough to believe this truth, however. We also need to be trained by it. If we want to move from fear to a hope that is founded in God's love and character, we need to walk the path articulated in Romans 5:2-5: "We rejoice in our sufferings, knowing

---

1. C.S. Lewis, *Mere Christianity* (London: Macmillan Publishers, 1952), 82.

that suffering produces endurance, and endurance produces character, and character produces hope, and hope does not put us to shame, because God's love has been poured into our hearts through the Holy Spirit who has been given to us." If we allow ourselves to be shaped by our difficulties—and don't hide away in fear—the challenges we face now will produce endurance, character, and hope in the long-term, and that hope will never be put to shame. We need to walk, full of faith, through challenging situations that could easily paralyze us with fear. We must not hide from God like Adam and Eve, nor bury our talents in the ground like the faithless servant. If we aren't paralyzed by fear, but rather buoyed by the love of God, we can be confident that we will be filled with hope.

As these verses in Romans suggest, this is not a "one and done" struggle. In fact, it is compounded for us in modern times, because today's world forces us to live in a state of constant change. This is particularly disconcerting to us as Westerners, because it defies our innate cultural tendencies to fall back into the need to categorize and control. In doing so, we risk losing sight of the mystery of God's beautiful work of redemption in our lives. Change can either drive us to fear when it causes us to throw our old paradigms out the window, *or* it can drive us to believe more deeply that we serve a God who won't be put in a box. He is infinitely creative, omnipotent, and most of all—as Susan learns in another of C.S. Lewis's classics, *The Lion, the Witch, and the Wardrobe*—He may not be *safe* (because he's a lion, after all!)[2] but He is most definitely *good*. The God who defines Himself as love (1 John 4:8) calls us not to seek safety but to move forward with faith in His goodness.

Called to Remember

One of the most formidable weapons in walking through difficult situations without fear, and allowing them to shape us toward hope, is the spiritual discipline of remembrance. Like prayer, fasting, and study, the spiritual disciplines have no power in and of themselves. As followers of Jesus Christ, indwelt by the Holy Spirit, we know that the

---

2. C.S. Lewis, *The Lion, the Witch and the Wardrobe* (NY: Harpercollins, 2004).

Spirit alone has the power to transform our hearts and minds and to conform us to the image of Christ (Galatians 6:8). And yet, as Richard Foster notes, spiritual disciplines are a vital means of "getting us into the ground"[3] and of posturing us for the Spirit to mold and shape us.

God constantly calls us to discipline our hearts to remember His love toward us, which He manifests throughout the arc of Scripture—creation, fall, redemption, and restoration. In the Old Testament, Yahweh constantly reminds the people of Israel through the prophets that "I led you up from Egypt and brought you out of the house of slavery. And I delivered you from the hand of the Egyptians and from the hand of all who oppressed you, and drove them out before you and gave you their land" (Judges 6:8-9). To seal the New Covenant, Jesus "took bread, and when he had given thanks, he broke it and gave it to them, saying, 'This is my body, which is given for you. Do this in remembrance of me'" (Luke 22:19). Jesus gives us the Holy Spirit, who "will teach you all things and bring to your remembrance all that I have said to you" (John 14:26). Remembrance brings assurance, comfort, and courage to face the unknown, our shortcomings, and our insecurities, all with the power that rose Jesus from the grave, power that is at our call. God wants us to remember over and over again that He is good, that He has called us to Him, that we are His. He wants us to remember who and whose we are.

As your authors, neither of whom started our careers in Christian schools, calling our own stories to remembrance brings hope. Lynn was a graduate professor of education at a secular university, a published author, conference speaker, and principal investigator for national-level grants. Providentially, her daughter's first-grade year at a Christian school coincided with a yearlong sabbatical. During that time, a new superintendent was hired. When he found out that Lynn had a background in education, he asked her to consider volunteering during his transition. Before her first official meeting with him in September, she prayed and thought hard about what skills she might be able to bring to the table. The only thing she could think of was accreditation, as she'd been involved in multiple accreditation efforts at the postsecondary level.

---

3. Richard Foster, *Celebration of Discipline* (San Francisco: Harper, 1998), 8.

When she told the superintendent, he stood up without a word, walked into another room, and returned with an office file box marked "Accreditation," which he then dropped—with a heavy thud—on the table in front of her. It turned out that in the midst of a multiyear leadership transition, the school hadn't filed an annual accreditation report in three years, and was within a month of losing its accreditation as a result. Overwhelmed with starting his new post and not having accreditation experience, the superintendent had been desperately praying for God to send someone who could get the school back on track. It was a "God moment" that couldn't be denied. Lynn took the task (and the box), and began a yearlong engagement with the school's major initiatives and areas in need of improvement.

When the university called the following April to plan her return, Lynn told them she wasn't coming back. This decision was scary, as it meant career suicide: walking away from leadership roles at her university and in her field nationally, hundreds of thousands of dollars in grant monies, and a highly coveted faculty position in education. But she had felt God's call to see the school through, having become personally invested in the faculty, the leaders, the students, and the families. And most of all, she felt deeply called to the hope of Christian education—to impact students not only for lifelong learning, but also for eternity. After nearly a decade of increasing responsibility and leadership at the school, she joined the Association of Christian Schools International (ACSI), first working with regional accreditation, then thought leadership and research, and then organizational planning and innovative strategy, including development of the Christian Education MindShift.

Jay not only didn't start out in Christian schools, he wasn't even in education. Instead, he was a practicing attorney with a young family and a baby on the way when God called him to a Christian school. Having recently been made a partner in his firm, he was just beginning to enjoy the fruits of nearly a decade of late nights, early mornings, weeks on the road, and weekends spent in trial preparation. September 11, 2001 came, and the resulting national trauma caused him to question the eternal value of what he then believed was his life's work. One month later, he received a "call out of the blue" from his church school's executive pastor, for the purpose of discussing an opening for a development director. Although Jay was sure at first that the pastor was just calling to ask for names of candidates he'd recommend, as he listened to the necessary qualifications and skills, Jay found himself realizing that he held many of them himself. He was stunned when the "ask" at the end of the conversation was not for candidate names, but a direct invitation for Jay to apply for the job.

Needless to say, this invitation was an unwelcome yet intriguing invasion on his life. With this invitation came profound fear of entering a field for which Jay had seemingly no life experience or preparation whatsoever, walking away from everything he had trained and worked for—as well as the prospects of major life adjustment brought on by a 70 percent pay cut, all with another child on the way. After much prayer and deliberation, Jay and his wife felt a deep calling to this new venture. But Jay still needed a confirming word from the Lord.

As Jay and his wife were driving in the car one day, they were discussing how deeply they believed God was calling them to make this move, as well as their apprehension of the profound change it would bring to their way of life. Their four-year-old daughter was traveling in the backseat, seemingly clueless to her parents' angst. From her car seat behind them, she pulled out her pacifier (she was too old—but don't judge!) and asked her daddy if he wanted to hear the Bible verse she had memorized in that same Christian school that was now calling him. He said, "Sure, honey." With her clear, tiny voice, she proclaimed, "Daddy, 'My God shall supply all your need according to His riches in glory by Christ Jesus,' Philippians 4:19." She then popped the pacifier back into her mouth, the Matthew 21:16 moment (praise ordained from the mouth of babes) being over. From that moment on, Jay stepped forward in faith, watching God provide richly moment after moment, and revealing that, veiled from Jay's eyes, every moment up until that moment had been preparation for God's call on his life.

For both of us, when the Author of Creation came calling, we had to listen. When as educators we are moved to make changes and shifts that are deeply rooted in who God has revealed His people, His image-bearers, to be; when we are called to undo decades of anti-normative pedagogical practices, brought about by broken educational training based upon faulty worldviews and defective college admissions algorithms that may have even yielded outward, pragmatic success yet visited potential harm on our students' very souls; when we are called to take a great risk to become better than we once were for the glory of God and the sake of His Kingdom and its children—our hope had better be resting in this God who has called the world into existence by His voice, who put death to death, and who has delivered each one of us, time and time again, and has promised us a hope and a future.

Case Story: Intentionally Left Blank

Between the two of us, we've visited over a hundred Christian schools and spoken with thousands of Christian educators in our travels. And without exception, all of these schools and educators have a unique but familiar story, in which fear (posed by potential loss, struggle, or challenge) was eclipsed by God's revelation to them that they are His dearly loved children in whom He is well pleased. Maybe your four-year-old daughter didn't prophesy to you, or you providentially weren't in the right place at the right time to rescue a school from losing accreditation. Or maybe it was something even more dramatic, like being healed from disease, or delivered from a situation in which there seemed to be absolutely no escape—except God. Yet, all the same, you remember the time—or really, all the times—when you were called to a great work, you trusted, and God provided. In those stories you can find encouragement afresh to place your hope in God's love and faithfulness and to move forward in courage despite your fear.

So what's next? Maybe you've heard a preacher say to turn to Acts Chapter 29, and you do so only to realize there is no 29th chapter (there are only 28, which means that chapter 29 is a metaphor for the story of God's activity that will be written through *your* life). This is that moment. You've reached the point where you—the reader—have to write your own case story. The next few pages are "intentionally left blank" so you can begin to record the story that God will weave into your life and the life of your school, as you prayerfully step out in faith, according to His leading.

Our parting encouragement is to start by writing a remembrance of who God is and how God delivered you when you trusted Him, not just once, but every single time. That will get you started and encourage you that you have every reason to trust God to help you as you continue writing your story, moment by moment. Remember that He never showed you His provision before you "stepped out of the boat," like the Apostle Peter (Matthew 14). It wouldn't be faith then, would it? You had to take the job, change the career, throw out the old plan, engage in the relationship, or launch the initiative before God showed you the plan. He did that so you would remember that your hope and trust were never in the job, the career, the person, or the plan—but in the One who loves you more than anyone else even has capacity to love, who has given you a hope and a future, and who guides every one of your steps as He leads you from fear to hope.

THIS PAGE INTENTIONALLY LEFT BLANK

THIS PAGE INTENTIONALLY LEFT BLANK

THIS PAGE INTENTIONALLY LEFT BLANK

THIS PAGE INTENTIONALLY LEFT BLANK

Epilogue: To Love is to Risk

Dan Beerens and Erik Ellefsen

Each author in this book loves Christian education. Many have taken a circuitous route in their personal lives to realize how deeply they love Christian education and why it matters so much to them. We wish you could hear each of their stories.

The authors of this book see Christian education as being threatened, and at the same time they see other ways that Christian education may continue to thrive. When something we love is threatened, we make choices. Deep love compels deep action. To love is to risk.

Consequently, the authors of this book have been students of outliers—those in other places risking and succeeding in doing something different and better. They see how we can fail in Christian education because we limit our vision and we limit the power of God. They realize it is time to step up and so have boldly shared their own "from…to" journeys, so that Christian education can continue to fulfill the noble goals to which it has always aspired.

Granted, it is a risk to try new things, to move in new directions, to love that deeply. But we have reached a time in history where by not innovating we are running a greater risk than staying our current course. Our fears are ever-present and division is a threatening possibility. But we know that we are not our own, that we rest in the truth that we serve at the calling of the King, and that this work is ultimately His.

To be sure, it feels better to risk together. The broad network of Christian educator friends engaged in MindShift, some of whom have shared their hearts and minds in this book, rely upon at least three things they hold in common:

1. A deep conviction that God is sovereign, and that we should respond back to God and neighbor with a deep faith through resting in His promises and seeking the guidance of His Holy Spirit;

2. A belief that it is better to walk the journey together with great companions, and that community is needed in order to challenge old assumptions, to ask difficult and sometimes uncomfortable questions, to urge each other on to better thinking, believing, and doing, and to pick each other up when inevitable discouragement sets in; and

3. A willingness to make the choice to see what is possible, what is good, right, and true, and to enjoy the journey—because we recognize that it is not ultimately our work, but rather we have been graciously invited to participate in the larger story of the Kingdom for such a time as this.

As we have internalized these truths, it has deeply affected how we as educators work—both together, and in our own contexts. These truths drive us to expend great offerings of time, energy, and resources in order to show Christ's love to our students, to our communities, and to each other.

We are inspired by great examples of selfless sacrifice by our predecessors in Christian education. Because of God's loving provision and their faithfulness, we are the grateful beneficiaries of today's Christian schools, programs, and organizations. As we have seen the examples, heard the stories, and read the book of Christian education history to this point, we suddenly realize that we are now writing the next chapter. The baton of the Christ story in education has been passed to us—and to you. Together, we all hold the responsibility and opportunity to respond proactively, to move into more biblically coherent ways of educating, and to offer our very best efforts back to our Creator as a sacrifice of praise, gratitude, and devotion.

About the Authors

Dan Beerens is an educational consultant, author, international speaker, and educational leader. Before starting Dan Beerens Consulting in May 2010, he served as Vice President of Learning Services and Director of Instructional Improvement at Christian Schools International. Prior to that, he was the Director of Curriculum and Instruction for Holland Christian Schools. Dan has also worked as teacher and principal in urban and suburban public and Christian schools in Wisconsin and Illinois. He serves as a Senior Fellow at the Center for the Advancement of Christian Education (CACE), represents Curriculum Trak sales and professional development, and serves as co-chair of the annual Christian Deeper Learning conference. He blogs regularly for CACE and is the author of *Evaluating Teachers for Professional Growth: Creating a Culture of Motivation and Learning* (Corwin Press, 1999).

Jenny Brady brings a unique perspective to the diversity discussion. Jenny is currently serving as the Director of Diversity for Prestonwood Christian Academy (PCA), a position created to express her passion for diversity while combining her personal experience growing up on the mission field in Honduras. She holds a Master of Science degree in Sociology and a BA in Spanish. In the educational realm, Jenny has worked as a teacher and administrator, is on the Leadership Team at PCA, and is currently participating in the Colson Fellows Program. She is the co-creator of the Christian School Diversity Symposium and is a speaker, teacher, and trainer on diversity for schools across the country. Jenny has a passion for missions and mentoring—taking the gospel to the ends of the earth while training up the next generation of godly young men and woman.

Dr. Michael Chen has been an educator for over 20 years in the San Francisco and Boston areas with experiences in urban education, international development, and organizational change. His career has included serving as dean of faculty at Boston Trinity Academy and the founding director of Trinity Institute for Leadership and Social Justice. Currently, he serves as the head of school at Pacific Bay Christian School. For his doctoral work, Michael developed a system-theory of resilience to further understand human development in the context of war-affected widows in Nepal. In addition, he also provided leadership and program evaluation consultative services to schools and organizations in South Korea, Nepal, and India.

After teaching in British Columbia, Toronto, and at his alma mater, Hamilton District Christian High School, **Justin Cook** is now with the Edvance Christian Schools Association as the Director of Learning, where he partners with 70 member schools in a vision of learning for flourishing communities. At home, Justin and his wife Rachel (and their three beautiful children) love trying to live intentionally in their neighborhood: sharing and restoring a multi-unit house, practicing hospitality, walking to church, and feasting with friends. Justin attended Redeemer University College and Calvin College and is currently an M.A. candidate at the Institute for Christian Studies in Toronto, ON.

Erik Ellefsen has served in education for 21 years as a teacher, coach, consultant, Grievance Chairman for the American Federation of Teachers, Dean of Academics at Boston Trinity Academy, and as Principal at Chicago Christian High School. He currently serves as an Academic and College Counselor at Valley Christian High School (San Jose, CA), a Senior Fellow for CACE, a Senior Fellow for Cardus, podcaster for Digical Education, and as Vice President of the Christian Coalition for Educational Innovation (CCEI). Erik regularly organizes Christian school leadership seminars and speaks on issues pertaining to academic programs, student leadership, and organizational development.

Jay Ferguson, J.D., PhD is the Head of School of Grace Community School in Tyler, Texas. Jay is in his 16th year as head of Grace. During that time, Jay has worked to build a flourishing culture at Grace, a vibrant educational community that has been awarded Blue Ribbon Exemplary status by the U.S. Department of Education in 2015 and 2017. He is an adjunct professor at Covenant College and at Gordon College and recently served on the adjunct faculties of the Van Lunen Center at Calvin College and Peabody College of Education at Vanderbilt University. Jay is currently President of the Board of the Texas Private School Association, the Chair of the Board of the Council on Educational Standards and Accountability (CESA), and serves on the executive board of the Association of Christian Schools International.

Joel Gaines serves as the high school principal at The City School in Philadelphia. He graduated from Philadelphia Biblical University (now Cairn University) with a BS in education and biblical studies, and he earned his MEd in education from Cabrini University. Joel has served in multiple roles over the past 10 years in both Christian and public schools and in both urban and suburban settings.

Dr. Beth Green, FRSA, is Visiting Professor: Research Integration and Educational Formation at Tyndale University College in Toronto. She is also a Senior Fellow at the faith-based think tank Cardus. Beth's expertise is in Christian school ethos; leadership and management; teaching and learning and social theory in education. At Cardus Education she led a program to enrich the public conversation with credible data on the impact of the religious school sector on graduate outcomes. Dr. Green is a former high school teacher and a graduate of Oxford, Cambridge, and London universities.

Dr. Keri D. Ingraham has served in Christian education the past 17 years in both the on-campus and online learning environments. Her experience includes head of school, administration, curriculum development, biblical integration, teaching, coaching, spiritual life leading, program development, and technology implementation. Currently, Dr. Ingraham is in her fourth year as the Director of PCA*plus* at Prestonwood Christian Academy in Plano, Texas where she is responsible for all aspects of the virtual academy, part-time on-campus program, and hybrid program. Her focus includes ensuring that PCA*plus* operates fully integrated with a Kingdom education philosophy, while moving PCA*plus* toward higher levels of excellence and innovation. She holds a Bachelor of Arts degree in Christian Educational Ministries from George Fox University, a Master of Education degree in Christian School Administration from Regent University, and a Doctor of Education degree in Christian Education Leadership from Regent University.

Dr. Darren Iselin is currently Executive Officer, National Tertiary Partnerships and Research, with Christian Schools Australia (CSA). Darren has over 25 years of leadership experience within Christian education, in Australian and international contexts, and has served in a diverse range of CEO, principal, and executive leadership roles and responsibilities in both K–12 schooling and higher education sectors. He has completed extensive formal study including doctoral work through the University of Queensland. Darren's award-winning research explored the sustainability of Christian school cultures in an era of change.

Rex Miller is the lead author for *Humanizing the Education Machine*, which tells the story of what great 21st-century learning looks like and how to bring that dynamic into schools. His company, MindShift, has tackled numerous large and complex problems, including the waste and adversarial culture of the construction industry and the chronic problem of workplace disengagement. His three books from these projects have won international awards for innovation and excellence. His current project examines ways to create healthy, less stressful, and more engaged schools (www.rexmiller.com).

Dr. Daniel Pampuch is Chief Executive Officer of Christian Schools Australia (CSA) overseeing 150 schools and 60,000 students. He was previously the Executive Officer of the Uniting Church Australia Schools and Residential Colleges Commission, overseeing 18 denominational institutions in Queensland. Daniel has 25 years of experience in Christian Education and most recently served as the Executive Principal of the CREST group of Christian schools and Early Learning Centres. Daniel has a PhD in Next Generation Leadership as well as Masters in Business, Education and Theology.

Daniel is passionate about research and in 2018 facilitated the Relational Schools Project in Australia where 20,000 students were surveyed to assess the impact that faith-based schools have upon student wellbeing and achievement. Daniel is a Fellow of the Governance Institute of Australia and a Fellow of the Institute of Managers and Leaders. He is a regular keynote speaker in leadership and lectures in organizational culture, governance, and theology.

Dr. Mitchell Salerno is Head of School at Monte Vista Christian School (MVCS) in Watsonville, CA. Mitch is the fifth head of school in the 93-year history of MVCS. He is a graduate of Wheaton College with a degree in chemistry, Duquesne University with master's in secondary education, and Liberty University with a doctorate in educational leadership. Mitch is the president of the Christian Coalition of Educational Innovation (CCEI), and a well-regarded speaker on topics including innovation, transformational leadership, and educational technology.

Dr. Justin Smith currently serves as Head of Upper School and Vice President at Little Rock Christian Academy. A graduate of the University of San Diego, Dr. Smith earned his doctorate in Educational Leadership from Sam Houston State University. With a number of published articles and peer-reviewed presentations on record, he also received such honors as the Excellence in Superintendency Program Award from Sam Houston State University and recognition as The Woodlands Preparatory School's Most Inspirational Educator. Additionally, Justin serves on the board of an independent boarding school outside of Philadelphia. Prior to leading at Little Rock Christian Academy, he served as Head of Middle School at Second Baptist School in Houston, Texas.

Dr. Lynn E. Swaner is the Chief Strategy and Innovation Officer at the Association of Christian Schools International (ACSI), where she leads initiatives to address compelling questions and challenges facing Christian education. Prior to joining ACSI she served as a Christian school administrator and a graduate professor of education. A published scholar, noted researcher, and conference speaker, she is the lead editor of the book *PIVOT: New Directions for Christian*

Education, co-author of *Bring It to Life: Christian Education and the Transformative Power of Service-Learning*, and editor of the ACSI blog. She received her EdD from Teachers College, Columbia University, in New York City.

Dr. Katie Wiens is the Executive Director of the Council on Educational Standards and Accountability (CESA). In her 20th year of education, Katie has diverse teaching and administrative experience in public and independent Christian schools in urban, suburban, and rural settings. Most recently she has worked at the University of Virginia alongside Dr. James Davison Hunter and a nation-wide team of researchers on a project investigating moral formation in 10 school sectors. In addition to her work at Boston Trinity Academy and Delaware County Christian School, Katie has taught at Wheaton College and Kennesaw State University and worked on the initial Christian Education Survey with Cardus.

Andy Wolfe is the Deputy Chief Education Officer (Leadership Development) for the Church of England, which runs nearly 5000 schools across England and educates over 1 million children. Andy has national oversight for the Church of England Foundation for Educational Leadership, which runs programs, networks, and research focused on leadership development. He joined the Foundation from the Nottingham Emmanuel School, where he worked for 10 years, initially as a middle leader, before being appointed Vice Principal, overseeing the development of Teaching and Learning and the school's Christian ethos. He brings a wealth of leadership experience to his senior role across the wider Church of England Education Office, and is committed to combining rich theological reflection with the most incisive and creative approaches to improving teaching, learning, and leadership in schools.